Italian Cooking

CLASSIC RECIPES

ANTONIETTA TERRIGNO

Italian Cooking – Classic Recipes

by

Antonietta Terrigno

Fourth Printing - Revised Edition – May 2005

Copyright © 1999 by
Antonietta Terrigno

Published by
Osteria de Medici
Unit 1, 201 - 10TH STREET N.W.
Calgary, Alberta
Canada   T2N 1V5
Phone: (403) 283-5553
Fax: (403) 283-5558
antonietta@osteria.ca
www.osteria.ca

National Library of Canada Cataloguing in Publication

Terrigno, Antonietta.
    Italian Cooking : great classic recipes / Antonietta Terrigno. — Rev. ed.

    Previous ed. has title: Antonietta's classic recipes.
    Includes index.
    ISBN 1-894022-80-7

1. Cookery, Italian.   I. Title. II. Title: Terrigno, Antonietta. Antonietta's classic
    recipes.

TX723.T37 2002   641.5945   C2002-911226-5

Photography by:
Patrick Cooney
1-800-813-5341
Calgary, Alberta

Designed, Printed and Produced in Canada by:
Bolder Graphics
5490 - 76 Ave SE., Calgary, Alberta T2C 4S3
1-800-313-6581   www.boldergraphics.com

This book is dedicated to my children
Maurizio and Michael,
and my husband
Rocco

INTRODUCTION

*A*ntonietta Terrigno, co-owner of Osteria de Medici in Calgary, has hosted some very famous people at her restaurant, including Pierre Trudeau, Sir Anthony Hopkins, Tom Selleck, Kevin Costner, Jane Goodall, Christopher Reeves, Cynthia Nixon, Loretta Swit, Andre Gagnon, Isabella Rossellini, Keith Carradine, Geena Rowlands, Steven Seagal and Jon Voight, all of whom appreciate the best in Italian cuisine.

Born in Molise, just east of Rome, Antonietta learned to cook with her mother at age 14, cooking everything from scratch and developing pride in serving only the best-quality food. Building on her heritage of generations of great Italian home cooks, she trained for five years in Rome and four years in Switzerland as a professional chef. In 1969 she married Rocco Terrigno, a schoolmate and chef who shared her passion for good food.

Their 27 years of restaurant experience is varied and extensive, including four years in St. Moritz. In 1976 they moved to Calgary, where their new restaurant, Osteria de Medici, has won many awards over the past 14 years. Their sons Maurizio and Michael are also part of their parents' professional lives and are involved in the restaurant.

Italian cuisine relies on the freshest fruits and vegetables, the best olive oil, seafood, meats, pasta and cheeses. This emphasis on freshness and quality, and the wide variety of vegetables used in Italian cooking makes it one of the healthiest cuisine choices in the world.

In her cookbook, Antonietta has chosen recipes that reflect the wonderful diversity of Italian cuisine, and she has used her experience and skill to simplify them for busy home cooks.

Italian cooking is loved and respected around the world. With Antonietta's cookbook everyone will feel confident about preparing these superb recipes for family and friends.

CONTENTS

FOREWORD

Superb flavor and simplicity are the best words to describe Antonietta Terrigno's *Italian Cooking – Classic Recipes.*

The flavors of Italy include famous ingredients like Parmigiano-Reggiano, Romano and mascarpone cheeses, Marsala wine, proscuitto, capicollo and extra-virgin olive oil. They include herbs like basil, rosemary, oregano and garlic. As you read through Antonietta's recipes the flavors and combinations of flavors stay in your mind. You can almost taste them.

Antonietta has taken great classic Italian recipes and used her skill as a chef to simplify them for home cooks. Her chapter on the basic sauces provides the foundation for many recipes. With these basics on hand, many of the recipes can be ready to eat in 20 to 30 minutes or less.

Building on her heritage of generations of great Italian cooks, Antonietta trained in Rome and in Switzerland as a professional chef. Her Calagry restaurant Osteria de Medici, has become famous with an international clientele for the outstanding quality of its cuisine. This striving for excellent quality and attention to detail are evident in her recipes.

It takes an outstanding chef to unravel the mysteries of culinary artistry. Antonietta has created a cookbook that can help new cooks become accomplished, and stimulate the inventive desires of accomplished cooks.

Many of these recipes will be reassuringly familiar to anyone who loves Italian food, many will be temptingly new. *Italian Cooking – Classic Recipes* is itself a classic, a cookbook to be trusted and treasured.

Ingredients of Great Italian Cooking

Popular Cheeses used in Classic Italian Cooking

Asiago - This cow's milk cheese has a pale yellow color and a nutty flavor. Aged Asiago hardens and is used grated.

Bocconcini - usually sold in containers with olive oil, water or whey, these small balls of fresh mozzarella have a light delicate flavor.

Caciocavallo - This cow's milk cheese from Southern Italy has a firm texture and mild flavor when young. The mature, aged cheese is suitable for grating and has a more pungent flavor. Smoked versions are also available. These cheeses are shaped like gourds and are tied around the "neck" with a string.

Gorgonzola - This cow's milk cheese from the Milan region is creamy and pungent, it is a superb blue table cheese. A great foil for grapes and pears, it can also be crumbled into salads and soups.

Friulano - This table cheese is sometimes called Italian Cheddar. It is firm with a buttery, nutty flavor.

Mascarpone - This very rich cow's milk cream cheese is from the Lombardy region. The buttery, delicate flavor is very suitable for desserts like Tiramisu, and for pairing with fruit.

Mozzarella - Originally made from water buffalo milk, this cheese is now made from cow's milk. The best fresh Italian mozzarella is available in containers with water or whey and has a more delicate flavor and texture than the usual commercial mozzarella.

Parmesan - Parmigiano-Reggiano is the correct name for the true aged Italian Parmesan from the Parma, Bologna, Modena region. Formaggi di grana *means cheeses with hard, grainy texture;* vecchio (old) *are aged 2 years,* stravecchio (extra-old) *are aged 3 years,* stravecchiones *are aged 4 years. Freshly grated Parmesan has an incomparable sharp, rich flavor.*

Pecorino - These cheeses are made from sheep's milk and may be aged (grana) or soft (ricotta). Aged pecorino Romano is grated and used in cooking. The flavor is sharp and rich.

Provolone Picante - Aged provolone can be grated and has a rich flavor. This cow's milk cheese comes southern Italy and is used for cooking.

Ricotta - This Italian version of cottage cheese has a fresh, delicate flavor. It is used in lasagne, other pasta dishes and cheesecakes.

Romano - This sheep's, goat's or cow's milk cheese is from Rome and has a milder flavor than Parmigiano-Reggiano. Aged Romano has a sharper flavor. It is grated and used for cooking.

HERBS

Basil is one of the most popular herbs and is commonly used in Italian cooking. Fresh basil can be cut up or chopped and kept in olive oil, ready to use whenever needed in soups, salads, sauces and in preparing meat and fish.

Rosemary is an aromatic herb that is excellent for roasted meats, marinades and savory breads.

Oregano when fresh is mild, sweet and aromatic and is excellent in fresh tomato sauces. Use dried oregano in moderation.

Garlic is the most widely used root herb in the world and is a major ingredient in all Italian cooking. Garlic is not usually used alone but works along with other ingredients to add a flavorful taste to a variety of foods.

MARSALA WINE

This wonderful aromatic wine comes from Marsala, Sicily. Most Italian families have a standard supply of Marsala wine in their pantry. Marsala comes in sweet and dry versions; always use sweet Marsala for cooking. Of the imported brands, Florio and Pellegrino, both produced in Marsala, are the best. Domestic Marsala should be used only if nothing else is available.

OLIVE OILS

Olive oil should have the greenish colour and fragrance of olives. It comes in three basic grades:

> **Extra-Virgin Oil,** made from olives that are not quite ripe, and is produced by stone crushing and cold pressing. Because it is produced without chemicals, it is of the highest quality and the most flavorful oil.

> **Virgin Olive Oil,** is produced the same way as extra virgin olive oil, but is made from olives that are more ripe.

> **Pure Olive Oil,** is the most common grade. It is produced by chemical means and contains only olive oils, without the blending of seed oil, hence the name "pure". The most common brands available in supermarkets are usually called "pure olive oil".

CAPICOLLO

Capicollo is a spicy ham-like seasoned cured meat made from pork neck. It is usually served thinly sliced as part of an antipasto tray.

PROSCIUTTO

Prosciutto is salted, air-cured ham. It is not smoked. It is widely used in Italian cooking and is often served as an appetizer with ripe figs or cantaloupe. Prosciutto is also added to pasta dishes as a flavorful garnish. Add it at the time of serving as it toughens when overcooked.

RICE

Italian rice (Riso) is short, high starch and thick grained. It is the perfect rice for the unique preparation of a delicious risotto. Years ago it was difficult to find Italian rice in most of North America. Today the best and most widely exported grain from Italy is Arborio. The high starch content contributes to the smooth texture of the perfect risotto.

STOCKS/BROTHS

Good broth is not only nourishing, but also an important element in Italian cooking. It is also vital to risotto and to innumerable soups. You will find a recipe for Chicken Broth on page 12.

TOMATOES

To prepare the perfect sauce, you need good quality tomatoes. The best tomatoes are grown in the southern regions of Italy.

WINE

Wine good enough for cooking should also be good enough to drink. Every ingredient you put into a dish affects its quality – wine is no exception. Using a little bit of good wine will improve the quality of your dish and your mood, as you will probably be sipping a little bit as you cook.

THE BASICS

Brodo Di Pollo

(Chicken Broth)

Soups and risottos are only as good as the broth or stock used to make them. This basic chicken stock will add rich flavor to your recipes.

1 lb. *(500 g)* chicken

2 celery stalks, chopped

1 medium onion, chopped

1 large carrot, chopped

salt & pepper to taste

5 quarts *(5 L)* water

Cut the chicken in half. Place the chicken, celery, onion, carrot, salt and pepper in a large saucepan. Add the water. Bring to a boil; reduce heat and simmer for 2 hours, removing the froth from the top with a slotted spoon.

Remove the chicken from the pot and reserve for use in other dishes.

Strain the broth through a fine sieve. Cool the broth, then cover and refrigerate.

Keep refrigerated or freeze in small containers. Broth will keep in the refrigerator for up to 5 days.

Makes 3 to 4 quarts *(3 to 4 L)*

Preparation Time: 15 minutes
Cooking Time: 2½ hours

Demi-Glace

Famed French chef Escoffier called demi-glace, "Sauce Espagnole taken to the extreme of perfection." This simplified version is very versatile, with intense flavor.

½ lb. *(250 g)* butter

½ lb. *(250 g)* all-purpose flour

64 oz. *(2 L)* canned beef broth or consomme

1 medium onion, chopped

1 carrot, chopped

1 celery stalk, chopped

4 bay leaves

3 garlic cloves, minced

1 tsp. *(5 mL)* black pepper corns

5½ oz. *(156 mL)* can tomato paste

*I*n a large pot, melt the butter; stir in the flour until smooth.

Add the remaining ingredients and bring to a boil. Reduce the heat and simmer for 2 hours.

Strain and use in sauces.

Cool and store in covered containers in the refrigerator or freezer.

Makes 2 quarts *(2 L)*

Preparation Time: **10 minutes**
Cooking Time: **2 ½ hours**

Beurre Manié

This butter and flour mixture is very useful for thickening savory sauces, gravies and soups. The name means "kneaded butter" in French.

¼ lb. *(115 g)* soft butter

¼ lb. *(115 g)* all-purpose flour

In a small bowl, mix butter and flour together until fully blended.

Use beurre manié to thicken soups and sauces. Stir in a little at a time until the sauce thickens. This butter mixture can be stored, refrigerated, for a long time.

Makes ⅔ cup *(150 g)*

Preparation Time: 10 minutes

Pastella

(*Batter for Deep-Frying*)

This batter is suitable for vegetables, chicken, shrimp, fish, etc. It makes a crispy, golden coating.

4 whole eggs

1 tbsp. *(15 mL)* baking powder

1½ cups *(375 mL)* flour

salt & pepper to taste

Mix eggs and baking powder together. Add flour a little at a time until the batter becomes fairly thick. Make sure the batter is smooth. Add salt and pepper.

Heat oil in a deep-fryer to 365°F (185°C). Dip desired items in the batter and fry until golden brown.

Makes 2 cups *(500 mL)* of batter

Preparation Time: 5 minutes
Cooking Time: 5-10 minutes

BESCIAMELLA SAUCE

(BÉCHAMEL SAUCE)

Also called Balsamella in Italy, this white sauce was invented by a courtier of Louis XIV's, Louis de Béchamel. It is one of the 4 "mother" sauces.

2 cups *(500 mL)* milk

¼ lb. *(115 g)* butter

½ cup *(125 mL)* flour

pinch salt & pepper

½ tsp. *(2 mL)* nutmeg

*H*eat the milk in a saucepan until it is very close to the boiling point. Set aside.

In another saucepan melt the butter over medium heat. When the butter has reached the frothing point add flour, salt, pepper and nutmeg. Stir well. Add hot milk slowly, stirring with a wire whisk or a wooden spoon (always stir in the same direction).

To prevent lumps from forming, lower the heat and let the sauce cook for 15 minutes, stirring frequently.

Makes 2 cups *(500 ml)*

Preparation Time: **5 minutes**
Cooking Time: **30 minutes**

Catherine de' Medici
(1519 - 1589)

When she was only 14 Catherine went to France to marry the future King Henry *II*. She brought with her, besides refined manners, many of the delicacies that were then enjoyed in Renaissance Italy: sweetbreads, truffles, artichoke hearts, quenelles of poultry, ice cream and frangipane tarts.

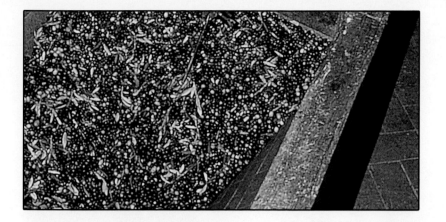

Prosciutto Con Melone (Prosciutto with Melon), Page 28

Lumache all'Anice (Snails with Anice), Page 35

MARGARITA

Born and raised in Mexico, the maragitas personality reflects the flavor of it's native land.

1 oz tequila

¼ oz triple sec

lime juice

Shake all ingredients together with ice. Strain into cocktail glass.

Pictured on page 21.

KIR ROYAL

A subtle blend of créme de cassis and champagne creates a wonderful taste sensation.

6 oz champagne

½ oz créme de casis

Pour champange into champagne glass. top with créme de cassis pouring very slowly, about ½ oz

Pictured opposite.

BÉARNAISE SAUCE

(TARRAGON BUTTER SAUCE)

Named for Béarn, Béarnaise sauce is delicious on cooked vegetables, roasted or grilled meats and fish. Tabasco and Worcestershire sauce add zest.

½ lb. (250 g) butter

4 egg yolks

¼ cup (60 mL) white wine

1 tbsp. (15 mL) chopped tarragon

1 lemon, juice of

dash Tabasco

dash Worcestershire sauce

salt & pepper to taste

Melt the butter in a small saucepan and set aside.

In a double boiler, over simmering water, whisk together the egg yolks and white wine until the mixture becomes fairly thick, but NOT like scrambled eggs. Remove from heat and let sit for about 1 minute.

Slowly whisk in butter, a little at a time, then whisk in the remaining ingredients.

Makes 2 cups (500 mL)

Preparation Time: **5 minutes**
Cooking Time: **5 minutes**

Ragu Bolognese

(Meat Sauce)

A specialty of Bologna, this hearty meat sauce is delicious with spaghetti and with heavier pasta shapes such as penne, fusilli and medium shells or bows. It is perfect for baked lasagne.

½ cup (125 mL) olive oil

1 green pepper, medium dice

1 onion, medium dice

1 celery stalk, diced

4 garlic cloves, minced

3.5 oz. (100 g) ground beef

7 oz. (200 g) ground pork

7 oz. (200 g) ground veal

2 quarts (2 L) canned tomatoes
   (2½, 28 oz. / 796 mL cans)

3 cups (750 mL) chicken broth,
   see page 12

1 tbsp. (15 mL) salt

1 tsp. (5 mL) pepper

Warm the oil in a very large skillet or in a large saucepan. Sauté the vegetables and garlic for 3 minutes.

Add the meat and cook for an additional 15 minutes.

Add tomatoes, broth, salt and pepper. Simmer for at least 2 hours, stirring occasionally.

Makes 2 quarts (2 L)

Preparation Time: 15 minutes
Cooking Time: 2 hours

Pictured on page 20.

Ragu Pomidoro

(Tomato Sauce)

If Béchamel is one of the "mother" sauces of French cooking, Tomato Sauce is one of the "mother" sauces of Italian cuisine. When garden tomatoes are available, use fresh tomatoes for the ultimate sauce.

½ cup (125 mL) olive oil

1 medium onion, diced

1 medium green pepper, diced

4 garlic cloves, minced

2 tbsps. (30 mL) salt

1 tsp. (5 mL) dried oregano

1 tbsp. (15 mL) black pepper

3 cups (750 mL) water

1 tbsp. (15 mL) minced fresh parsley

6 lbs. (2.8 kgs) canned, crushed tomatoes (3½, 28 oz. / 796 mL cans)

Warm the olive oil in large skillet; add onion, pepper and garlic; sauté for 5 minutes.

Add the rest of the ingredients.

Cook the sauce for 2 hours at a low temperature, stirring occasionally.

Serve this sauce with any seafood, pasta or veal dish.

Makes 2 quarts (2 litres) of sauce

Preparation Time: 20 minutes
Cooking Time: 2-3 hours

APPETIZERS

PROSCIUTTO CON MELONE

(PROSCIUTTO WITH MELON)

The salty tang of prosciutto is perfect with the mellow sweetness of cantaloupe. This is a true classic (see page 10).

2 cantaloupes

12 thin slices of prosciutto

*P*eel and slice each cantaloupe into 6 slices.

Place 3 slices of cantaloupe on each of 4 plates and lay a slice of prosciutto on each cantaloupe slice.

Serves 4

Preparation Time: 5 minutes

*Variation: Substitute ripe figs for the cantaloupe.

Pictured on page 19.

Mozzarella In Carrozza

This classic Italian dish gave rise to fried Mozzarella.

2 eggs

2 cups flour

2 cups bread crumbs, finely grated

2 cups olive oil

pinch of salt and pepper

6 balls of Bocconcini

Whip eggs with the salt and pepper.

Dip the Bocconcini in the flour first, then in the egg mixture, finishing in the bread crumbs.

Cook in hot oil until golden brown.

Serves 6

Preparation Time: 10 minutes

BRUSCHETTA

Bruschetta is grilled or toasted bread rubbed with garlic, drizzled with olive oil and sprinkled with salt and pepper. A traditional appetizer or accompaniment, the addition of this tomato, garlic topping makes it irresistable.

TOMATO & GARLIC TOPPING

10 medium tomatoes, finely diced

1 tsp. *(5 mL)* black pepper

1 tsp. *(5 mL)* salt

1 tbsp. *(15 mL)* chopped oregano

4 garlic cloves, minced

½ cup *(125 mL)* olive oil

¼ lb. *(115 g)* soft butter

4 shallots, finely chopped

10 Italian dinner rolls, cut in half

Topping: Mix all ingredients together in a large bowl. Cover and refrigerate overnight.

Preheat oven grill. Combine butter and the shallots. Spread shallot butter on bread and place on a baking sheet. Place rolls in oven and grill until the bread is browned.

Spoon topping onto toasted bread and serve.

Serves 6 to 10

Preparation Time: 15 minutes
Cooking Time: 5 minutes

Pictured on page 39.

GARLIC CROSTINI

Crostini means little toasts in Italian. These garlic flavored little toasts are easy to make and very versatile.

¼ cup *(60 mL)* olive oil

2 garlic cloves, minced

1 baguette, cut in 1" *(2.5 cm)* slices

Preheat oven to 375°F (190°C). Combine oil and garlic in a small bowl.

Place baguette slices on a baking sheet. Brush the tops of the bread slices with the oil and garlic mixture. Bake for 10 minutes or until lightly toasted.

Serve with dips and spreads.

Makes 32 Crostini

Preparation Time: 5 minutes
Baking Time: 10 minutes

GRISSINI CON FUNGHI

(BRANDIED SAUTÉED MUSHROOMS ON TOAST)

Brandy and cream add luxurious flavor to sautéed mushrooms.

1 tbsp. *(15 mL)* olive oil

1 clove garlic, crushed

4 cups *(1 L)* sliced mushrooms

1 tsp. *(5 mL)* salt

1 tsp. *(5 mL)* pepper

1 cup *(250 mL)* whipping cream

2 oz. *(60 mL)* brandy

8 slices toast

In a small saucepan, heat oil and sauté garlic. Add sliced mushrooms, salt, pepper and whipping cream. Reduce heat and stir until thickened.

Spoon the mushrooms on the toast and serve.

Serves 8

Preparation Time: 30 minutes
Cooking Time: 25 minutes

ANTIPASTO DI GAMBERETTI

(SHRIMP COCKTAIL)

This all-time favorite appetizer is presented with a zesty brandy-horseradish sauce.

6 cups (1.5 L) water

salt

1 lemon, juice of

30 large fresh shrimp, peeled, deveined

COCKTAIL SAUCE WITH BRANDY

2 cups (500 mL) ketchup

½ cup (125 mL) brandy

2 tbsp. (30 mL) horseradish

2 tsp. (10 mL) salt

1 tsp. (5 mL) pepper

1½ cups (375 mL) shredded lettuce

*I*n a large saucepan, bring water to a boil. Add salt and half of the lemon juice. Add shrimp and cook over medium heat till the flesh turns completely white, about 5 minutes. Drain and let cool.

*S*auce: Mix together the ketchup, brandy, horseradish, salt and pepper.

When ready to serve, place lettuce in the bottom of 6 champagne glasses. Top with sauce and hang 5 shrimp over the rim of each glass.

Serves 6

Preparation Time: 15 minutes
Cooking Time: 5 minutes

Antipasto Frutti Di Mare

(Cold Seafood Appetizer)

Fresh seafood is readily available along Italy's coasts so Italians enjoy a magnificent array of delicious seafood dishes.

1 lemon, juice of

8 medium scallops

3-6 squid

8 shrimp

16 mussels

1 tsp. *(5 mL)* each salt, black pepper

¼ cup *(60 mL)* red wine vinegar

1 cup *(250 mL)* diced red pepper

1 cup *(250 mL)* diced green pepper

½ cup *(125 mL)* olive oil

1 tsp *(5 mL)* dried oregano

fresh parsley sprigs

1 lemon, cut in wedges for garnish

In a large saucepan, bring water and lemon juice to a boil. Add all of the seafood and boil for 5 minutes; drain and cool. Season with salt and pepper.

In a medium saucepan, bring 2 cups (500 mL) of water and the vinegar to a boil. Add the peppers and boil for 10 minutes; cool. Add the oil and oregano.

Divide the seafood among 4 plates. Spoon the pepper mixture over the seafood. Garnish with fresh parsley and lemon wedges.

Serves 4

Preparation Time: 20 minutes
Cooking Time: 15 minutes

Pictured on page 41.

Antipasto Alla Marinara

(Seafarer's Antipasto)

Garlic, lemon and zesty hot sauces complement the delicate fresh flavors of shrimp, scallops and calamari.

SEAFOOD

1 lb. *(500 g)* squid (calamari), cleaned* and sliced crosswise, 3/4" thick

1 lb. *(500 g)* scallops, sliced ½" *(1.5 cm)* thick

1 lb. *(500 g)* raw shrimp in shell

1 lemon, juice of

ZESTY OIL & GARLIC DRESSING

2 garlic cloves, minced

2 tbsp. *(30 mL)* fresh parsley, finely chopped

1 cup olive oil

1 lemon, juice of

dash Worcestershire sauce

dash Tabasco sauce

salt & pepper to taste

lettuce for garnish

*S*eafood: Slice scallops; wash shrimps (leaving them in the shell); clean squid and slice. Bring a large saucepan of salted water to a boil. Add seafood and lemon juice. Boil until cooked, about 5 minutes. Remove from the heat and let the seafood cool in the water. Once cooled, drain the seafood and peel the shrimp.

*D*ressing: Combine garlic, parsley, oil, lemon juice, Worcestershire sauce, Tabasco sauce, salt and pepper. Mix well.

Combine the seafood with the dressing. Marinate for 20 minutes or more. Serve on a bed of lettuce.

Serves 6

Preparation Time: 15 minutes
Cooking Time: 30 minutes

* To clean squid (this is best done over a sink), peel off the skin from the body section. Pull the head and tentacles away from the body sac. Cut the tentacles from the head and discard the head and any intestines attached. Remove the translucent quill from the body sac and discard the quill and intestines. There is a hard beak at the base of the tentacles, remove and discard it. Under cold running water, rinse the tentacles and body sac well. Drain well.

LUMACHE ALL'ANICE

(SNAILS WITH ANISE)

The licorice flavor of anise is a lovely addition to this rich buttery sauce.

ANISE BUTTER

3 garlic cloves, minced

1 pearl onion, finely chopped

2 tbsp. *(30 mL)* finely chopped fresh
  parsley

¾ cup *(175 mL)* butter, softened

3 oz. *(90 mL)* anisette liqueur*

36 snails

Prepare the anise butter by mixing together all of the ingredients in a small bowl.

Place the snails in snail dishes and cover each snail with Anise Butter.

Bake at 400°F (200°C) for 10 minutes, or until the butter is bubbling. Serve immediately.

Serves 6

Preparation Time: 10 minutes
Cooking Time: 10 minutes

* Pernod, pastis or ouzo are all anise-flavoured liqueurs that may be substituted for anisette.

Pictured on page 19.

Lumache Al Forno Con Pernod E Aglio

(Baked Snails with Pernod & Garlic)

Pernod adds a subtle licorice flavor, similar to the absinthe that inspired many of the Impressionists.

Escargot Butter

½ cup butter, melted

½ cup Pernod

1 green onions

1 garlic clove

1 tsp. Worcestershire sauce

salt & pepper to taste

chopped parsley

butter

24 escargot

*I*n a small saucepan, warm the butter. Stir in the remaining Escargot Butter ingredients.

To serve, place a dab of regular butter in each escargot shell or use escargot dishes. Place a washed escargot in each shell and pack with Escargot Butter.

Bake at 425°F (220°C) for a few minutes, just until hot.

Serves 4

Preparation Time: 10 minutes
Cooking Time: 10 minutes

Calamari Fritti

(Deep-Fried Squid)

This classic Mediterranean appetizer has become extremely popular in North America. Deservedly so! Cooked properly, fresh squid is tender and slightly sweet.

2½ lbs. *(1.25 kg)* fresh squid

2 cups *(500 mL)* milk

1 cup *(250 mL)* flour

2 cups *(500 mL)* vegetable oil

salt

lemon wedges

Slice the body of the squid crosswise into ¾" (2 cm) thick slices. Cut the tentacles into bite-sized pieces if they are large.

Dry the squid pieces; then drop them in milk and then in flour, to coat lightly.

In a large skillet, heat oil until it is very hot, about 365°F (185°C). Carefully add the squid, turning to cook both sides. Cook just until the squid is crispy. Drain on paper towels. (If you overcook squid it will be too tough to eat. Squid should be slightly raw in the middle.)

Sprinkle squid with salt and garnish with lemon wedges.

Serves 4 to 6

Preparation Time: 10 minutes
Cooking Time: 10 minutes

* See the note about cleaning squid on page 34.

Marinated Salmon & Blini

Blini are the classic accompaniment to marinated or smoked salmon, or caviar. Traditional blini are small pancakes made with yeast. This simple version is light and delicious.

MARINATED SALMON

4 lb. *(2 kg)* salmon fillet, no bones, skin on (approximately 1 side of salmon)

2 tbsp. *(30 mL)* chopped fresh dill

2 tbsp. *(30 mL)* chopped fresh parsley

¾ cup *(175 mL)* rock salt

1 cup *(250 mL)* Demerara sugar

2 oz. *(60 mL)* dark rum

2 tbsp. *(30 mL)* freshly squeezed lemon juice

1 bay leaf

6 peppercorns, crushed

BLINI

1¼ cups *(300 mL)* buckwheat flour

⅔ cup *(150 mL)* flour

2 tsp. *(10 mL)* sugar

½ tsp. *(2 mL)* baking powder

1 cup *(250 mL)* milk

2 eggs

¼ cup *(60 mL)* sour cream

¼ cup *(60 mL)* butter, melted

Place the salmon skin-side down in an acid-proof pan (glass, enamel or stainless steel). Combine remaining ingredients in a blender until blended well. Pour over salmon; marinate for 48 hours in the refrigerator, turning every 12 hours.

Blini: Combine flours, sugar, baking powder and pinch salt. Combine milk and eggs. Add alternately with sour cream to dry ingredients. Mix until smooth. Add butter and blend. Pour onto a greased baking sheet. Bake at 325°F (160°C) for 25 minutes. Cut into 50 pieces.

Remove the salmon from the marinade and remove excess seasoning and residue. Slice the salmon as thinly as possible. Serve cold with Blini.

Yields 50 portions

Preparation Time: Salmon, 10 minutes
Blini, 10 minutes
Marinating Time: 48 hours
Cooking Time: 25 minutes

Torta Al Formaggio

(CHEESECAKE)

This savory cheesecake has a glazed fruit topping – serve it with red wine as an appetizer or as a cheese course for dessert.

2 tbsp. *(30 mL)* unsalted butter

1 garlic clove, minced

½ cup *(125 mL)* plain bread crumbs

¾ cup finely chopped *(175 mL)* walnuts

¼ tsp. *(1 mL)* salt

16 oz. *(455g)* cream cheese, softened

8 oz. *(225g)* Parmesan cheese, grated

2 eggs, separated

¼ cup *(75 mL)* + 1 tbsp. heavy cream

2 tsp. *(10 mL)* dry mustard

½ tsp. *(2 mL)* white pepper

1 tbsp. *(15 mL)* cornstarch

1 ½ tbsp. *(22 mL)* finely minced shallots

pinch of cream of tartar

GLAZED FRUIT TOPPING

2 tbsp. unsalted butter

3 shallots

1 small tart green apple, sliced, with peel

6 dried figs, quartered

grated zest of 1 orange and juice of ½ the orange

⅓ cup chopped walnuts

⅓ cup dried cherries

⅓ cup apple jelly

Grease an 8" (20 cm) springform pan. Set aside.

To make the crust, melt butter in a large skillet. Add garlic and cook briefly. Stir in bread crumbs, walnuts and salt until well mixed. Cool. Press over the bottom of the pan.

With an electric mixer, in a large bowl blend cheeses until smooth. Add egg yolks, 1 at a time, until blended. Add cream while mixing. Add mustard, pepper, cornstarch and shallots. Blend until smooth.

In a separate bowl, beat egg whites with cream of tartar until stiff, but not dry. Fold gently into the cheese mixture. Spoon into the pan and spread evenly.

Bake at 325°F (160°C) for 1 hour. Turn off oven and leave cake inside, without opening the door, for 1 hour. Remove cake and cover with a damp towel. Cool to room temperature. Top with Glazed Fruit.

Glazed Fruit Topping: Melt the butter in a sauté pan and sauté shallots until soft. Add apples, figs, zest, juice, walnuts and cherries and simmer on low until apples are just tender. Spoon over the cake.

Heat the jelly in a small pan on low heat until just melted. Brush over the fruit as a glaze. Serve the cake at room temperature.

Serves 12

Preparation Time: 30 minutes
Cooking Time: 1 hour

BRANDY SCALLOPS

Scallops are light dishes traditional in Italian cooking from Rome.

16 large scallops, sliced

3 oz brandy

2 tbsp. *(30 mL)* olive oil

1 tbsp. *(15 mL)* chopped parsley

1½ cup *(450 mL)* 35% cream

salt & pepper to taste

Saute scallops for 5 min on medium high heat in olive oil. Season with salt & pepper and remove from stove top. Deglaze pan with brandy, using caution as brandy may flame up. Add cream, return to heat, reduce to medium-low and let sauce reduce and thicken. Garnish with chopped parsley. Serve hot with crusty italian bread.

Serves 4

Preparation Time: 15 minutes
Cooking Time: 25 minutes

SOUPS

Capellini In Brodo

(Angel Hair with Broth)

Capellini is a delicate, thin pasta, also called capelli d'angelo. It gives an ethereal quality to this Italian chicken noodle soup.

1 lb. *(500 g)* angel hair pasta

3 quarts *(3 L)* chicken broth*, see page 12

salt & pepper to taste

Cook angel hair pasta in 2 quarts (2 L) of salted boiling water for 3 to 5 minutes.

Meanwhile, bring the broth to a boil and season with salt and pepper to taste. Strain the pasta and add it to the broth. Ladle into bowls.

Serves 6

Preparation Time: 5 minutes
Cooking Time: 10 minutes*

* Prepare the chicken broth when you have ample time and freeze or refrigerate it until needed.

Pictured on page 40.

Zuppa Di Spinaci

(Spinach Soup)

Fresh spinach has a wonderful tart, slightly bitter flavor that is mellowed with the rich salty flavors of chicken broth and Parmesan cheese. There is no cream in this soup so it has a more intense flavor and a lovely color.

2 lbs. *(1 kg)* fresh spinach

4 cups *(1 L)* water

2 quarts *(2 L)* chicken broth, see page 12

2 garlic cloves, minced

½ cup *(125 mL)* grated Parmesan cheese

salt & pepper to taste

Wash the spinach and remove the stems. Place the spinach in a large saucepan with the water and simmer until just limp, 1 to 2 minutes. Drain the spinach and chop finely. Set aside.

In a large saucepan, combine chicken broth, garlic, salt, pepper and cooked spinach. Bring to a boil. Reduce the heat and add Parmesan cheese. Simmer for 30 minutes and remove from the heat.

Serves 6

Preparation Time: 15 minutes
Cooking Time: 45 minutes

Bruschetta, page 23

Zuppa Di Scarola

(Curly Endive Soup)

In North America curly endive is sometimes called chicory. The lacy, green outer leaves with curled tips grow in loose heads. Their tart flavor adds zest to this garlicy soup.

3 heads of curly endive, coarsely chopped

3 quarts *(3 L)* chicken broth, see page 12

3 garlic cloves, minced

1 tsp. *(5 mL)* salt

1 tsp. *(5 mL)* black ground pepper

1 tbsp. *(15 mL)* chopped parsley

*I*n a large saucepan, cook the endive in salted boiling water for approximately 10 minutes. Drain off the water.

Chop the endive and return it to the pot. Add the broth with the garlic, salt, pepper and parsley. Simmer for 30 minutes.

Serves 6

Preparation Time: 10 minutes
Cooking Time: 40 minutes

Zuppa Di Zucchini Con Riso

(Zucchini & Rice Soup)

The rich colors of zucchini and tomato add eye appeal to this hearty soup.

1 small onion, finely chopped

1 garlic clove, minced

1 tbsp. *(15 mL)* butter

3 tbsp. *(45 mL)* vegetable oil

3 zucchini, coarsely diced

2 medium fresh tomatoes

2 quarts *(2 L)* chicken broth, see page 12

1½ cups *(375 mL)* rice

salt & pepper to taste

grated Parmesan cheese

*I*n a large saucepan, sauté onion and garlic in butter and oil. Add zucchini and tomatoes, stirring well. Simmer for 45 minutes.

Add broth, rice, salt and pepper. Bring to a boil. Reduce heat and simmer until rice is tender, about 20 minutes. Stir frequently.

Sprinkle with grated Parmesan cheese and serve.

Serves 4

Preparation Time: 30 minutes
Cooking Time: 1 hour

MINESTRONE

Every family has their favorite recipe for this traditional hearty Italian soup. Almost any combination of seasonal vegetables can be used. It can also contain beans or peas or pasta, and is often topped with Parmesan cheese.

⅓ cup (*75 mL*) olive oil

1 large zucchini, diced

1 medium carrot, diced

1 medium onion, diced

8 celery stalks, diced

3 peeled potatoes, diced

½ cup (*125 mL*) chopped prosciutto

2 cups (*500 mL*) whole stewed tomatoes

2 quarts (*2 L*) chicken broth, see page 12

½ cup (*125 mL*) cooked spinach

salt & pepper to taste

*H*eat the oil in a large saucepan and sauté the zucchini, carrots, onion, celery and potatoes with the prosciutto for approximately 10 minutes.

Add the stewed tomatoes and continue cooking for another 10 minutes.

Add the broth and cook until vegetables are soft, about 20 minutes.

Add the spinach, salt and pepper just before serving.

Serves 6

Preparation Time: 20 minutes
Cooking Time: 40 minutes

Stracciatella Alla Romana

(Chicken Soup with Egg)

A classic Roman soup, Stracciatella has a slightly curdled texture from the beaten eggs and cheese. The aroma is heavenly, as is the flavor.

3 eggs, beaten

½ cup *(125 mL)* grated Parmesan cheese

1 tbsp. *(15 mL)* finely chopped fresh parsley

4 cups *(1 L)* chicken broth, see page 12

*I*n a small bowl, beat together the eggs, Parmesan cheese and parsley. Set aside.

In a medium saucepan, bring the chicken broth to a boil on high heat. Pour in the egg mixture. Simmer for 5 minutes (do not stir).

Remove from the heat and serve.

Serves 4

Preparation Time: 5 minutes
Cooking Time: 8 minutes

Zuppa Di Lenticchie

(Lentil Soup)

Lentils add rich earthy flavor to soups and stews, Their high nutritional value and low fat content has made them very popular in contemporary North American recipes, but Mediterranean cooks have used them for centuries.

½ lb. (250 g) dried lentils

2 quarts (2 L) water

2 medium potatoes, quartered

2 tbsp. (30 mL) vegetable oil

1 tsp. (5 mL) butter

1 small onion, finely chopped

1 small carrot, finely chopped

1 celery stalk, finely chopped

1 garlic clove, minced

2 strips bacon, finely chopped

7½ oz. (213 mL) can plum-style Italian tomatoes

salt & pepper to taste

Soak the lentils for 6 hours or overnight in cold water to cover. Drain lentils and discard the water.

Place the lentils in a large saucepan with the potatoes and cover with water. Bring to a boil, reduce heat and cook until lentils and potatoes are tender, about 20 to 30 minutes. Drain and save the liquid.

In another saucepan, heat the oil and butter and sauté the onion, carrot, celery, garlic and bacon. Add peeled tomatoes and the lentil liquid. Simmer for half an hour.

Remove the potatoes from the lentils and mash the potatoes. Return the potatoes to the lentils and add the tomato mixture. Add salt and pepper. Bring to a boil and simmer for 5 minutes before serving.

Serves 6 to 8

Preparation Time: 20 minutes
Cooking Time: 1 hour

Pasta E Fagioli

(Italian Bean Soup)

In Italy the savory thick peasant bean soups are full of flavor and good nutrition. This soup has accents of garlic, rosemary and sage.

4 cups *(1 L)* dried beans (white or brown)

1 medium carrot, diced

1 medium onion, diced

1 large green pepper, diced

1 lb. *(500 g)* chopped prosciutto

4 quarts *(4 L)* chicken broth, see page 12

3 garlic cloves, minced

1 tsp. *(5 mL)* dried rosemary

1 tsp. *(5 mL)* dried sage

3 cups *(750 mL)* whole stewed tomatoes

4 cups *(1 L)* cooked macaroni (2¼ cups / *550 mL* raw macaroni)

salt & pepper to taste

Soak the beans overnight in water to cover. Drain. Discard the water.

Sauté the beans and other vegetables in a large saucepan with the prosciutto. Add the chicken broth. Cook until the beans become soft and the soup thickens, about 2½ hours.

In a small saucepan, lightly brown the garlic, rosemary and sage. Add this to the soup.

Add the cooked macaroni and season with salt and pepper. Reheat and serve.

Serves 8

Preparation Time: 45 minutes
Cooking Time: 3 hours

Zuppa Pavese

(Poached Eggs in Broth)

This delicate soup is unusual in that the eggs are poached in the serving bowls by the boiling broth. This soup is very attractive in appearance.

1½ quarts *(1.5 L)* chicken broth, see page 12

4 eggs

1 cup *(250 mL)* croûtons

4 tbsp. *(60 mL)* grated Parmesan cheese

*I*n a medium saucepan, bring chicken broth to a boil. Reduce heat and simmer.

Carefully break 1 egg into each of 4 soup bowls and top with croûtons and 1 tbsp. (15 mL) of Parmesan cheese.

Pour a cup (250 mL) of broth over each egg and serve immediately.

Serves 4

Preparation Time: 5 minutes
Cooking Time: 5 minutes

CREMA DI POLLO

(CREAM OF CHICKEN SOUP)

Just a hint of cream adds rich flavor to this simple and flavorful soup.

1 lb. *(500 g)* chicken

2 celery stalks, coarsely chopped

1 medium onion, coarsely chopped

1 large carrot, peeled, coarsely chopped

salt & pepper to taste

4½ quarts *(4.5 L)* water

1 cup *(250 mL)* butter

1 cup *(250 mL)* flour

2 egg yolks

¼ cup *(60 mL)* whipping cream

Cut the chicken in half and place in a stock pot with the celery, onion, carrot, salt and pepper, and water. Bring to a boil. Reduce heat and simmer for 2 hours, occasionally skimming the froth from the top.

Remove the chicken, bone and chop the meat finely. Set aside. Strain and reserve the chicken broth.

Melt the butter in a large saucepan over medium heat. Gradually add flour, stirring well.

Add 2-quarts (2 L) chicken broth and simmer over low heat for about half an hour, stirring occasionally.

Remove from the heat and add the chopped chicken, egg yolks and whipping cream, stirring well for about 5 minutes. Serve immediately.

Serves 6

Preparation Time: 15 minutes
Cooking Time: 2½ hours

Zuppa Di Pesce

(Fish Soup)

Like the famed bouillabaisse of Provence this magnificent fish and shellfish soup is flavored with saffron, garlic and herbs. Unlike bouillabaisse, the broth is served with the fish, but separately.

4 lbs. *(1.8 kg)* assorted fresh fish, cut in large pieces (conger, eel, perch, turbot, red mullet)

1 lb. *(500 g)* assorted shellfish, leave in shell (clams, baby lobster, shrimps, mussels, scallops, crab legs)

1 cup *(250 mL)* vegetable oil

28 oz. *(796 mL)* peeled tomatoes, chopped fine and save liquid

1 onion, chopped fine

1 leek (heart only), chopped fine

1 garlic clove, minced

pinch of zafferano (saffron)

1 tsp. *(5 mL)* thyme

2 cups *(500 mL)* wine

3 quarts *(3 L)* chicken broth, see page 12

4 cups *(1 L)* croutons

Wash and clean all fish and shellfish. Place the seafood in a large pot and add all of the remaining ingredients, except the wine, chicken broth and croûtons. Mix well and let marinate for 2 to 3 hours, stirring occasionally.

Place the saucepan on the burner and cook over high heat for 15 minutes. Stir frequently. Pour the wine and broth over the seafood and continue cooking for another 10 minutes. Reduce heat. Stir well.

Remove from heat. Remove the seafood and place on a platter. Place croûtons in each soup bowl and pour the broth over the croûtons. Serve the soup with the fish.

Serves 10 to 12

Preparation Time: 45 minutes
Cooking Time: 4 hours

SALADS

SALADS

1. When washing lettuce, squeeze the juice of 1 or 2 lemons into the water and add about ½ tsp. (2 mL) salt. The lemon juice adds to the crispness of the lettuce, and the salt will drive out any insects hidden in the lettuce leaves.

2. If the lettuce seems to be limp, add ice cubes to the water and allow the lettuce to soak a few minutes.

3. After a thorough washing, dry the lettuce thoroughly between towels or drain well in a salad basket.

4. Always chill lettuce after it is cleaned. Put it in a cloth bag or other closed container in a refrigerator to keep it cold and crispy.

5. If you wish tomatoes to be added to a salad, prepare them separately and use them as garnish. If they are added with the other ingredients, their juices will thin the dressing.

6. It is best to cut tomatoes in vertical slices because they bleed less this way.

7. A tastier tossed salad will result if several kinds of lettuce are used.

8. Always taste a tossed salad before serving. If it seems dull, add a little more vinegar or salt and pepper.

9. Chill salad plates (bowls), especially if serving individual salads.

10. For a change of pace, try chilling the salad forks, too. You'll be amazed at the reactions you'll receive.

INSALATA DI VEDURE MISTE

(MIXED SALAD)

This mixed vegetable salad includes fennel (finocchio), which is very popular in Italy, both raw and cooked. Raw fennel imparts a delicate, slightly sweet licorice flavor; cooked fennel has a more subtle mild flavor.

½ head of butter lettuce

1 small head of curly endive

1 celery stalk, sliced thick

2 fennel bulbs, sliced ½" (1.3 cm) thick

3 small radishes, thinly sliced

2 tomatoes, quartered

oil & vinegar

salt to taste

Discard the outer leaves from the greens. Wash the greens quickly and pat dry with towels. Tear into bite-sized pieces and place in a large salad bowl.

Slice the celery, fennel, radishes and tomatoes and add to the salad. Season with salt and add just enough oil to coat all of the ingredients. Sprinkle with vinegar and toss gently.

Serves 6

Preparation Time: 10 minutes

INSALATA DI ARANCE

(ORANGE SALAD)

Very refreshing and attractive, this salad makes a wonderful palate cleanser between courses, or serve with heavier meat dishes for contrast.

6 oranges

1 tbsp. *(15 mL)* olive oil

1 tsp. *(5 mL)* salt

pepper to taste

Peel the oranges and slice them into rounds. Add the oil, salt and freshly ground pepper.

The orange slices may be arranged on individual serving plates or served from a salad bowl.

Serves 4 to 6

Preparation Time: 5 minutes

Insalata D'Arance & Belga

(Orange & Endive Salad)

*The mild flavor of Belgian endive is a very good contrast to the sweet tang of oranges.
The Lemon Dijon Dressing adds just the right amount of sharpness.*

4 small bunches of Belgian
    endive*

3 oranges

Lemon Dijon Dressing

1 tbsp. *(15 mL)* Dijon mustard

½ cup *(125 mL)* oil

1 lemon, juice of

salt & pepper to taste

Discard outer leaves from the endive. Wash the endive quickly and thoroughly in cold water and dry. Tear into bite-sized pieces and place in a large salad bowl.

Peel the oranges and split them into sections; add to greens.

Combine mustard, oil, lemon, salt and pepper. Mix well. Pour over the salad and toss gently. Serve immediately.

Serves 4 to 6

Preparation Time: 10 minutes

* Because Belgian endive becomes bitter when exposed to light, store it wrapped in paper towels, in a plastic bag, in the refrigerator. Look for endive with firm, tight heads and crisp leaves, with pale yellow tips.

Caesar Salad

Even though this salad originated in Mexico, it was, of course, an Italian chef who created this new Italian classic.

1 head of romaine lettuce

Caesar Dressing

4 egg yolks

5 garlic cloves

1 tbsp. *(15 mL)* capers, chopped

3 anchovy filets, chopped

½ tsp. *(2 mL)* dry mustard

1 cup *(250 mL)* olive oil

2 lemons, juice of

dash Tabasco sauce

dash Worcestershire sauce

salt & pepper to taste

1 cup *(250 mL)* croûtons

½ cup *(125 mL)* Parmesan cheese

Wash romaine and tear into bite-sized pieces. Store in a cloth towel.

Dressing: In a medium bowl, combine egg yolks, garlic, capers, anchovy and mustard. With an electric mixer, beat on high until smooth. With mixer running, slowly add olive oil, mixing until the oil is completely absorbed. Then add lemon juice, Tabasco sauce, Worcestershire sauce, salt and pepper.

In a large salad bowl, combine lettuce, croûtons and Parmesan. Add the dressing and toss well.

Serves 8

Preparation Time: 20 minutes

INSALATA DI POMODORO

(TOMATO SALAD)

The first Italian tomatoes were golden in color, so they were called pomodoro – golden apples. Fresh garden tomatoes need no other dressing than this basil-accented oil and vinegar.

6 ripe tomatoes

salt to taste

1 garlic clove, minced

1 tsp. *(5 mL)* dried oregano

6 fresh basil leaves, chopped

½ cup *(125 mL)* olive oil

¼ cup *(60 mL)* red wine vinegar

Wash and slice the tomatoes. Place the slices on a platter in 1 layer.

Sprinkle the tomatoes with salt, garlic, oregano and basil. Pour olive oil over tomatoes and sprinkle with red wine vinegar.

Let stand for about 10 minutes before serving.

Serves 6

Preparation Time: 5 minutes

INSALATA DI FAGIOLINI

(GREEN BEANS WITH TOMATOES)

This colorful salad is at its best when fresh garden tomatoes are available.

1 lb. *(500 g)* fresh green beans

2 ripe tomatoes, quartered

½ cup *(125 mL)* olive oil

1 lemon, juice of

salt & pepper to taste

Trim beans and cut into 1" (2.5 cm) pieces. Cook beans in boiling salted water until tender, about 10 minutes. Drain and cool.

In a large bowl, combine beans, tomatoes, oil, lemon juice, salt and pepper. Mix well.

Serves 4

Preparation Time: 20 minutes
Cooking Time: 10 minutes

INSALATA DI BOCCONCINI E POMIDORO

(FRESH CHEESE & TOMATO SALAD)

Usually marinated in whey, mild bocconcini is a fresh mozzarella with a special affinity for tomatoes.

6 medium tomatoes

6 bocconcini cheese balls

HERBED BALSAMIC DRESSING

1 cup *(250 mL)* olive oil

½ cup *(250 mL)* balsamic vinegar

1 tsp. *(5 mL)* salt

1 tsp. *(5 mL)* pepper

1 tsp. *(5 mL)* dried oregano

1 tsp. *(5 mL)* dried parsley

Slice tomatoes and bocconcini cheese crosswise.

In a bowl, mix together the other ingredients.

Arrange tomato and cheese slices on individual plates and pour dressing over the top.

Serves 6

Preparation Time: 5 minutes

INSALATA DI PEPERONI

(ROASTED PEPPER SALAD)

Roasting peppers softens them and adds a delicious mellow smoky flavor.

6 large sweet bell peppers, green &
red

1 garlic clove, minced

¼ cup *(60 mL)* olive oil

salt to taste

Preheat oven to 400°F (200°C). Lay whole peppers on a baking sheet and place in the oven for about 20 minutes. Turn peppers frequently so the skin will be evenly roasted (skin should blister).

Remove peppers from the oven and let cool for about 10 minutes.

Peel the peppers and remove the stems and seeds.

Cut the peppers into thin strips and place them in a serving dish. Add garlic and oil. Season with salt and mix well. Let stand for about an hour before serving.

Serves 4 to 6

Preparation Time: **15 minutes**
Cooking Time: **20 to 30 minutes**

Insalata Di Zucchini

(Marinated Zucchini Salad)

The small zucchini have the best flavor and are the most attractive in presentation. Using a combination of green and gold zucchini is less traditional but it looks lovely.

2 small zucchinis, cleaned and cubed

3 medium tomatoes, chopped

1 small red onion, chopped

2 tbsp. *(30 mL)* chopped fresh basil

1 tbsp. *(15 mL)* olive oil

2 tbsp. *(30 mL)* balsamic vinegar

½ tsp. *(2 mL)* freshly ground pepper

Place zucchini in a medium saucepan, add water to cover and bring to a boil. Cook for 2 to 4 minutes, until just tender; cool.

In a non-metal bowl, combine all ingredients. Refrigerate a minimum of 2 hours before serving.

Serves 6

Preparation Time: 20 minutes
Chilling Time: 2 hours

INSALATA DI FINOCCHIO

(FENNEL SALAD)

The mild licorice flavor of fennel is the starring feature of this simple salad.

---

4 heads of fennel, sliced

½ cup olive oil

salt & pepper to taste

---

*T*o prepare the fennel, separate the stalks, cut them off the base and discard. Trim the fennel bulb, removing as little as possible. Quarter or halve the bulb lengthwise and slice thinly.

Combine all ingredients in a large bowl and mix well.

Serves 6

Preparation Time: 10 minutes

* Fennel discolors quickly when exposed to the air. Rub cut surfaces with lemon if arranging fennel in a salad before dressing it.

PASTA

Before Marco Polo went to the valley "Del Katai", pasta had been known for hundreds of years. Instead of spaghetti it was called rishta, an Arabic word. Noodles are thought by archaeologists to date back to 3000 B.C. or earlier in China and Japan. In Italy, in Etruscan tombs, pasta rolling and cutting tools have been found that date back to 400 B.C. When Marco Polo returned to Venezia, Italy in the 13th century, he brought with him wheat flour. It was used to make spaghetti and bread.

The pasta was prepared on a large wooden table, mixed by hand, and hydrated with underground well water. To make pasta thin, wooden tubes were used to wrap the dough mixture around, thus creating thin pieces of pasta. Various styles of pasta were developed, for example, some were cut shorter for use in soups.

The Medici family taught the people of Florence how to cook pasta and how to eat it with a fork and spoon. Today, there are hundreds of pasta shapes, sizes and colors, from the standard macaroni, spaghetti, fettuccine, linguine and lasagne, to orzo (small rice-grain shapes) to delicate capelli d'angelo (angel hair), conchiglie (ridged conch shells), farfalle (butterflies), tagliatelle (long, flat egg noodles), fusilli (spirals), penne (pen-nib shapes), radiatore (squat rectangles with rippled edges), etc. Colored pastas add even more variety to the amazing range of shapes. Tomato paste is used for red pasta, spinach for green and squid ink for black.

In Italian, pasta with sauce is called "La Pastasciuttas".

Cooking Pasta

Knowing how to cook pasta is very important in Italian cuisine. To cook pasta you need a generous amount of salted water. A good rule is about 4 times the amount of water to pasta. For example, for 1 lb. (500 g) of penne you would need 2 quarts (2 L) of water and 2 tbsp. (30 mL) of salt. Make sure the water comes to a boil before adding the pasta, and always stir the pasta to prevent it from sticking. When pasta is done it should be al dente, soft and slightly firm to the bite. Then strain the pasta and serve with the desired dish or sauce.

Pasta Fresca Con Uova

(Egg Pasta)

Egg pasta is used mainly for flat noodles. Homemade pasta is superb, you owe it to yourself to try the real thing.

1 ½ cups (375 mL) unsifted all-purpose flour

1 egg

1 egg white

1 tbsp. (15 mL) olive oil

1 tsp. (5 mL) salt

few drops water

*P*our the flour into a large mixing bowl or in a heap on a pastry board. Make a well in the center of the flour and in it put the egg, egg white, oil and salt. Mix together with a fork or your fingers until the dough can be gathered into a rough ball. Moisten any remaining dry bits of flour with drops of water and press them into the ball.

To make pasta by hand: knead the dough on a floured board, working in a little extra flour if the dough seems sticky. After about 10 minutes the dough should be smooth, shiny and elastic. Wrap the dough in waxed paper and let it rest for at least 10 minutes before rolling it.

Divide the dough into 2 balls. Place 1 ball on a floured board or pastry cloth and flatten it with the palm of your hand into an oblong about 1" (2.5 cm) thick. Dust the top lightly with flour. Then, using a heavy rolling pin, start at one end of the oblong and roll it out lengthwise, away from you, to within 1" (2.5 cm) or so of the farthest edge. Turn the dough crosswise and roll across its width. Repeat, turning and rolling the dough, until it is paper thin. If at any time the dough begins to stick, lift it carefully and sprinkle more flour under it.

To make cannelloni, tortellini, page 87, and ravioli, page 88, follow the cutting directions in those recipes.

A pasta machine will do both the kneading and rolling. Pull off about ⅓ of the dough at a time, set the smooth rolls of the pasta machine as far apart as possible and feed the piece of dough through them. Re-roll this strip 4 or 5 more times, folding under the ragged edges and dusting the dough lightly with flour if it feels sticky. When the dough is smooth, shiny and elastic, it has been kneaded enough. Now start to roll it out, setting the machine to the second notch and feeding the dough through with the rolls closer together. Then set the machine at the third notch and roll the dough thinner. Repeat, changing the notch after each rolling, until the dough is about $1/16$" (1.5 mm) thick.

Makes about ¾ lb. (340 g).

LASAGNE

Lasagne has become a world-wide favorite. It is true comfort food, hearty, delicious and satisfying.

PASTA DOUGH

6 whole eggs

2 lbs. *(1 kg)* all-purpose flour

---

2 quarts *(2 L)* meat sauce, see page 19

1½ lbs. *(700 g)* grated mozzarella cheese

2 cups *(500 mL)* grated Parmesan cheese

*P*asta: Mix egg and flour together until it forms a nice smooth dough. Let stand for 2 hours. Using a pasta machine, roll out about 10 sheets to 8" (20 cm) in length. Cook them in boiling water and cool. If using dry pasta use the same process.

In a 9 x 13" (23 x 33 cm) baking pan, place a little of the meat sauce on the bottom, then place 2 or 3 of the cooked lasagne noodles on the top. Pour in a little more meat sauce and place grated mozzarella cheese and Parmesan cheese on top. Repeat this process until the layers reach the top of the pan, finishing with a layer of cheese.

Bake at 350°F (180°C) for 30 to 40 minutes.

Lasagne Serves 6
Pasta Dough Makes 10, 8" (20 cm) lasagne noodles

Preparation Time: 30 minutes
Cooking Time: 30 minutes to 1 hour

LASAGNE ROLL-UPS

These decorative roll-ups combine a herbed tomato sausage sauce with a three-cheese spinach filling – exquisite!

TOMATO SAUSAGE SAUCE

1 lb. *(500 g)* Italian sausage meat

½ cup *(125 mL)* chopped onion

1 garlic clove, crushed

1 ⅓ cups *(325 mL)* tomato paste

1 ⅔ cups *(400 mL)* water

1 tsp. *(5 mL)* dried oregano

½ tsp. *(2 mL)* dried basil

SPINACH CHEESE FILLING

10 oz. pkg. *(283 g)* frozen chopped spinach (thawed and drained well)

2 cups *(500 mL)* ricotta cheese

1 cup *(250 mL)* Parmesan cheese

1 ½ cups *(375 mL)* mozzarella cheese

1 egg slightly beaten

½ tsp. *(2 mL)* salt

¼ tsp. *(1 mL)* pepper

6 Lasagne noodles, cooked

Remove the sausage from the casings. Crumble sausage and sauté with onion and garlic in a medium saucepan. Pour off excess fat. Add tomato paste, water, oregano and basil. Cover; simmer gently for 20 minutes.

In a medium bowl, combine spinach, ricotta cheese, Parmesan cheese, 1 cup (250 mL) mozzarella cheese, egg, salt and pepper and mix well.

Spread about ½ cup (125 mL) of the cheese mixture on each lasagne noodle; roll up, Place the rolled noodles seam-side down in a 8 x 12" (20 x 30 cm) baking dish. Pour the meat sauce over the rolls. Top with the remaining ½ cup (125 mL) mozzarella cheese.

Bake at 350°F (180°C) for 30 minutes, or until heated through.

Serves 4 to 6

Preparation Time: 30 minutes
Cooking Time: 1 hour

LASAGNE CON FRUTTI DI MARE

(SEAFOOD LASAGNE)

An elegant seafood lasagne, this superb dish is creamy yet light and can be adapted to your favorite combination of seafood.

9 lasagne noodles

16 oz. (475 g) light ricotta

1/2 cup (125 mL) grated Parmesan cheese

1/3 cup (75 mL) table cream (18% mf)

WHITE SAUCE

1/2 cup (125 mL) butter

2 cups (500 mL) chopped fennel

1 onion, chopped

1/2 cup (125 mL) all-purpose flour

4 cups (1 L) milk

1 lb. (500 g) cooked seafood (shrimp, scallops, lobster, clams or mussels)

1 cup (250 mL) shredded mozzarella cheese

*I*n a large pot of salted, boiling water, cook lasagne noodles for 10 to 12 minutes, or until tender. Rinse under cold water, drain and set aside.

In a bowl, stir together ricotta, Parmesan and cream; set aside. In a large, heavy-bottomed saucepan, melt butter over medium heat. Add fennel and onion; reduce heat to medium-low and cook for 10 minutes, or until softened. Add flour and cook 1 minute, stirring constantly. Gradually add milk, whisking constantly. Bring to a boil over medium heat, stirring constantly. Reduce heat to low and simmer 10 minutes or until thickened, stirring occasionally. Remove 1 cup (250 mL) of the white sauce and set aside. Add seafood to simmering sauce and cook 30 seconds, or until seafood is slightly warmed, stirring constantly.

Spread 1/4 cup (60 mL) of the reserved white sauce in a 9 x 13" (23 x 33 cm) baking dish. Layer with 3 lasagne noodles. Spoon half of the seafood sauce on top of the noodles. Layer with 3 more lasagne noodles. Spoon remaining seafood sauce on top and cover with the last 3 lasagne noodles. Pour remaining 3/4 cup (175 mL) of reserved white sauce on top and sprinkle with mozzarella. Bake at 350°F (190°C) for 25 minutes, or until heated through and mozzarella is melted.

Serves 12

Preparation Time: 20 minutes
Cooking Time: 1 hour

Gnocchi Alla Romana

(Dumplings Roman Style)

These delicious dumplings are traditionally served with butter and Parmesan as a side dish. They may also be served with savory sauces.

4 cups (*1 L*) milk

2 ½ cups (*600 mL*) coarse semolina* (*300 g*)

1 tbsp. (*15 mL*) butter

1 tbsp. (*15 mL*) olive oil

Parmesan cheese

3 egg yolks

salt & pepper to taste

1 tbsp. (*15 mL*) butter

½ cup (*125 mL*) Parmesan cheese, or more to cover

*I*n a medium saucepan, bring milk to a boil and whisk in semolina. Add butter and oil. Let cook for 30 minutes on low. Stir in cheese and egg yolks until smooth. Spread the dough 1" (2.5 cm) thick on an oiled baking sheet and cool in the refrigerator.

Cut the dough into circles with a cup. Grease a 9 x 13" (23 x 33 cm) baking dish with the butter and place the gnocchi on top. Sprinkle with cheese.

Bake at 350°F (180°C) for 20 minutes.

Serves 8

Preparation Time: 5 minutes
Cooking Time: 1 hour

* Semolina is a coarse durum wheat flour, often used to make pasta.

Maccheroni Gratinati Al Forno

(Baked Macaroni)

Macaroni and cheese has topped many polls of favorite foods in North America. This Italian version is pure comfort food.

1 lb. *(500 g)* large elbow macaroni

¼ cup *(60 mL)* butter

½ cup *(125 mL)* grated Parmesan cheese

2 cups *(500 mL)* Besciamella Sauce, see page 15

In a large saucepan, bring 2 quarts (2 L) of water to a boil. Add 2 tbsp. of salt. Add the macaroni, boiling until partially cooked, about 5 minutes.

Drain the macaroni and return it to the pot. Mix in butter and Parmesan cheese.

Place the macaroni in a shallow 3-quart (3 L) baking dish and cover with Besciamella Sauce.

Bake at 350°F (180°C) for 30 minutes, or until the top is golden brown and crispy.

Serves 6

Preparation Time: 10 minutes
Cooking Time: 30 minutes

Rigatoni Al Forno

(Baked Rigatoni)

When you have meat sauce on hand, this hearty baked pasta dish is simple to make and full of flavor.

1 lb. *(500 g)* rigatoni*

1 cup grated Parmesan cheese

1 lb. *(500 g)* mozzarella cheese, grated

2 quarts *(2 L)* meat sauce, see page 19

8 slices mozzarella cheese

*I*n a large saucepan of boiling, salted water, cook the pasta until al dente, 12 to 16 minutes. Drain.

In a saucepan, heat the meat sauce.

Mix the sauce with the pasta and the grated mozzarella and Parmesan cheeses. Place in a shallow 3-quart (3 L) baking dish and place the sliced cheese on top.

Bake at 450°F (230°C) for 5 minutes, until the top is browned.

Serves 4

Preparation Time: 20 minutes
Cooking Time: 25 minutes

* Rigatoni are shaped like large macaroni tubes, with a grooved/ribbed surface.

Spaghetti Al Forno

(Baked Spaghetti)

Beautiful presentation and memorable flavor, this baked spaghetti "pie" is also easy to prepare.

10 oz. *(285 g)* spaghetti, cooked

Meat Sauce

1 tsp. *(5 mL)* dried basil or thyme

1 lb. *(250 g)* lean ground beef

1 garlic clove, crushed

1 tsp. *(5 mL)* dried oregano or Italian seasoning

1 onion, chopped

salt & freshly ground pepper to taste

2 cups *(500 mL)* tomato sauce, see page 20

¼ cup *(60 mL)* chopped green pepper

1 cup (250 mL) shredded mozzarella cheese

*I*n a large pot of boiling, salted water, cook the spaghetti for 7 to 8 minutes, until al dente. Drain

Toss 4 cups (1 L) of the cooked spaghetti with basil or thyme and press over the bottom and up the sides of a 10" (25 cm) glass pie plate.

Meanwhile, in a skillet, brown ground beef with garlic, oregano, onion, salt and pepper. Drain off any excess fat. Add spaghetti sauce and green pepper. Simmer for 2 to 3 minutes.

Pour the meat sauce into the center of the spaghetti "crust." Garnish with additional browned ground beef, if desired. Cover loosely with foil and bake at 450°F (230°C) for 5 minutes. Top with the mozarella.

Let stand, covered, for 5 minutes before serving. Cut into wedges and serve with a tossed salad.

Serves 4 to 6

Preparation Time: 20 minutes
Cooking Time: 10 minutes

Spaghetti Aglio E Olio

(Spaghetti in Garlic and Oil)

Very simple and very good, the flavor of the extra-virgin olive oil marries with the garlic in a perfect fusion of flavors.

1 lb. *(500 g)* spaghettini or linguine

6 garlic cloves, minced

⅓ - ½ cup *(75-125 mL)* extra-virgin olive oil

salt & freshly ground pepper to taste

½ cup *(125 mL)* freshly grated Parmesan cheese

Cook the pasta in 2 quarts (2 L) of boiling, salted water for 4 to 5 minutes.

While the pasta is cooking, heat the garlic in ⅓ cup (75 mL) of olive oil in a frying pan over low heat. When the mixture just begins to bubble, stir and cook for a few more minutes, until the garlic just begins to turn golden. Do not let the garlic brown.

When the pasta is partially cooked, drain it and add to the frying pan; toss well. Season to taste with salt and pepper, adding a bit more oil if you like.

Serve immediately with Parmesan cheese.

Serves 4

Preparation Time: 10 minutes
Cooking Time: 10 minutes

Linguine Alla Vongole

(Linguine with Clam Sauce)

Wine and garlic are a fragrant and flavorful combination in this light clam sauce. The pinch of chilies adds zest.

Clam Sauce

2 lbs. *(1 kg)* fresh baby clams in their shells, or 5 oz. *(140 g)* can

½ cup *(125 mL)* olive oil

2 garlic cloves, minced

pinch of crushed chilies

pinch of oregano

5 sprigs parsley, finely chopped

1 cup *(250 mL)* dry white wine

---

1 lb. *(500 g)* linguine

Wash and scrub fresh clams several times.

In a large skillet, heat the oil and sauté the garlic. Cook over medium heat until garlic turns light brown. Add the remaining sauce ingredients and cover the pot. When the clams have opened, remove them from the shells and return them to the skillet. Simmer the clams for 5 minutes, stirring occasionally.

In a large pot of boiling, salted water, cook the linguine for 4 to 5 minutes, until just al dente. Drain the pasta and add to the clam sauce. Mix well. Remove from the heat and serve.

Serves 6

Preparation Time: **10 minutes**
Cooking Time: **15 minutes**

* When using canned clams, add clams and liquid to garlic along with the seasonings and wine. When cooking clams in their shells, discard any clams that do not open.

Fusilli Principessa

(Fusilli with Asparagus)

The height of luxury, asparagus, mushrooms, brandy and cream, this sauce is incredibly easy to make and outrageously good.

1 lb. *(500 g)* fusilli*

4 tbsp. *(60 mL)* butter

1 cup *(250 mL)* sliced mushrooms

2 cups *(500 mL)* chopped asparagus tips

¼ cup *(60 mL)* brandy

2 cups *(500 mL)* cream

salt & pepper to taste

½ cup *(125 mL)* grated Parmesan cheese

*I*n a large saucepan of boiling salted water, cook the pasta for 10 to 12 minutes.

In a separate, large saucepan, melt the butter and sauté mushrooms and asparagus. Add brandy and cream. Reduce heat and cook until the sauce starts to thicken. Add salt and pepper.

Stir in the cooked pasta. Stir in the Parmesan cheese.

Serves 4

Preparation Time: 10 minutes
Cooking Time: 15 minutes

Pictured on page 94.

* Fusilli is a spiral (spring-shaped) pasta about 1 ½" (4 cm) long.

Fettuccine Al Burro E Panna

(Fettuccine Alfredo)

THE CLASSIC – this smooth rich sauce is fabulous. Created in Rome in the 1920s, it has become a favorite around the world. Freshly ground black pepper is a must for this sauce.

8 tbsp. *(120 mL)* unsalted butter

1 cup *(250 mL)* heavy cream

2 tbsp. *(30 mL)* salt

1 lb. *(500 g)* fresh fettuccine

1 cup *(250 mL)* freshly grated
   Parmesan cheese

freshly ground pepper

*I*n a large saucepan, bring 2 quarts (2 L) of water to a boil.

As the water for the pasta begins to boil, melt the butter in large sauté pan over low heat. Add the cream to the butter and let it warm.

At the same time, salt the water and cook the pasta until al dente, about 7 to 9 minutes.

Drain the pasta and mix thoroughly with the butter and cream, over low heat. Add the cheese and toss until the sauce thickens slightly. Season with the pepper. Serve immediately and pass additional cheese at the table.

Serves 4 to 5 people

Preparation Time: 15 minutes
Cooking Time: 15 minutes

Bucatini Alla Rafrano

(Pasta with Horseradish)

Horseradish and garlic add zest to this unusual pasta dish. There is no sauce, so it is very dry.

½ lb. (*500 g*) bucatini*

¼ cup (*60 mL*) butter

2 garlic cloves crushed

¼ cup (*60 mL*) grated fresh
   horseradish

¼ cup (*60 mL*) bread crumbs

¼ cup (*60 mL*) Parmesan cheese

Cook the pasta in boiling salted water until it is al dente, 12 to 15 minutes.

Meanwhile, melt the butter in a saucepan and sauté the garlic. Drain the pasta and add it to the pan, stir in the remaining ingredients and serve.

Serves 6

Preparation Time: 10 minutes
Cooking Time: 10 minutes

* Bucatini is a hollow pasta, just a bit thicker than spaghetti, that comes in long strands. A thicker version is called bucatoni.

Spaghetti Con Mozzarella E Tomatoes

(Spaghetti with Mozzarella & Tomatoes)

Fresh and fantastic – these flavors are intense and pure. This uncooked sauce is a superb summer treat when fresh basil and fresh tomatoes are at their peak.

3 tomatoes, diced

1½ cups (375 mL) cubed mozzarella cheese

2 garlic cloves, minced

½ cup (125 mL) packed fresh basil leaves, finely chopped

1 tsp. (5 mL) pepper

½ tsp. (2 mL) salt

2 green onions, finely chopped

¼ cup (60 mL) extra-virgin olive oil

¾ lb. (340 g) spaghetti

freshly ground black pepper

*I*n a large bowl, stir together tomatoes, mozzarella cubes, garlic, basil, pepper, salt and green onions. Drizzle with oil and toss to combine. Let stand 30 minutes.

Meanwhile, in a large pot of boiling, salted water, cook pasta 8 to 10 minutes, until al dente. Drain pasta and toss immediately with marinated tomato mixture. Serve with freshly ground black pepper.

Serves 4

Preparation Time: 10 minutes
Cooking Time: 10 minutes
Marinating Time: 30 minutes

Capellini Alla Marinara

(Angel Hair Pasta & Tomato Sauce)

The salty tang of anchovies adds zest to this garlicky herbed tomato sauce.

2 garlic cloves, minced

2 anchovy filets

1 tbsp. *(15 mL)* olive oil

½ medium onion, diced

1 tsp. *(5 mL)* dried oregano

1 tsp. *(5 mL)* dried parsley

1 quart *(1 L)* tomato sauce, see page 20

salt & pepper to taste

1 lb. *(500 g)* capellini (angel hair)

½ cup *(125 mL)* grated Parmesan cheese

Crush the garlic and anchovy together until a paste forms.

In a large saucepan, heat the oil and sauté the onions and garlic/anchovy paste until the onions are translucent.

Add oregano and parsley, followed by the tomato sauce, salt and pepper. Cook for 5 minutes over medium heat.

Meanwhile, cook the pasta in a large pot of boiling, salted water for 3 to 4 minutes.

Drain the pasta and add to the sauce. Add the cheese.

Serves 4

Preparation Time: 5 minutes
Cooking Time: 15 minutes

Linguine Alla Puttanesca

(Linguine with Olives & Capers)

This spicy sauce from Naples has a fabulous fragrance and flavor. It is named after the "ladies of the night" who reputedly created it for its energy-boosting powers.

28 oz. *(796 mL)* can tomatoes

2 tbsp. *(30 mL)* virgin olive oil

2 x 2 oz. *(50 g)* cans anchovy fillets, drained, and finely chopped (optional)

4 garlic cloves, minced

½ cup *(125 mL)* sliced, pitted, medium, ripe olives

½ cup *(125 mL)* sliced, stuffed manzanilla olives

2 tbsp. *(30 mL)* drained capers

½ tsp. *(2 mL)* hot pepper flakes

¼ tsp. *(1 mL)* dried oregano

¼ tsp. *(1 mL)* salt

¾ lb. *(340 g)* linguine

¼ cup *(60 mL)* chopped fresh Italian parsley

Place tomatoes and juice in food processor. Pulse on and off until tomatoes are crushed; set aside.

In a large skillet, heat olive oil over medium heat. Add anchovies (if using), garlic, olives, capers, hot pepper flakes, oregano and salt. Cook for 3 minutes, or until garlic softens, stirring constantly. Stir in tomatoes; cook for 20 minutes, or until the sauce thickens.

Meanwhile, in a pot of boiling, salted water, cook the pasta for 6 minutes, or until al dente. Drain well. Toss with the sauce and fresh parsley. Serve immediately.

Serves 4

Preparation Time: 10 minutes
Cooking Time: 25 minutes

TORTELLINI

(PASTA RINGS STUFFED WITH CHICKEN AND CHEESE)

These "little twists" of pasta are similar to cappelletti "little hats". They may have a variety of savory fillings.

CHICKEN & CHEESE FILLING

2 ¼ cups (550 mL) finely chopped, cooked chicken (3 single chicken breasts, boned & skinned, & poached in stock for 15 minutes)

½ cup (125 mL) freshly grated Parmesan cheese

2 egg yolks, lightly beaten

⅛ tsp. (0.5 mL) grated lemon peel

⅛ tsp. (0.5 mL) ground nutmeg

salt

freshly ground black pepper

---

pasta dough, see page 61, double the recipe

6 to 8 quarts (6 to 8 L) water

salt

Thoroughly combine the chicken, cheese, egg yolks, lemon peel and nutmeg in a large bowl. Season with salt and pepper.

Break off ¼ of the pasta dough, and keep the rest moist by covering with foil or a damp cloth. Roll out the dough on a floured board until it is paper thin, then cut into 2" (5 cm) rounds with a biscuit cutter or a small glass.

Place ¼ tsp. (1 mL) of the chicken mixture in the center of each round. Moisten the edges of each round. Fold the circles in half and press the edges firmly together. Shape into little rings by stretching the tips of each half circle slightly and wrapping the ring around your index finger. Gently press the tips of the circle together. The tortellini are best if they are cooked at once, but they may be covered with plastic wrap and refrigerated for a day or so.

Bring the water and salt to a boil in a heavy pot or kettle. Drop in the tortellini and stir gently with a wooden spoon for a moment to make sure they do not stick to one another. Boil, stirring occasionally, for about 8 minutes, or until they are tender. Drain the tortellini in a large sieve or colander. Serve with Ragu Bolognese, page 19, or in hot beef or chicken stock.

Makes about 80 / Serves 8 to 10

Preparation Time: 1 hour
Cooking Time: 10 minutes

RAVIOLI

These tempting pillows of pasta dough may be stuffed with a variety of fillings.

RICOTTA & PARMESAN FILLING

1½ cups (*375 mL*) ricotta

¾ cup (*175 mL*) freshly grated
   Parmesan cheese

2 tsp. (*10 mL*) grated onion

3 egg yolks

1½ tsp. (*7 mL*) salt

VEAL & SPINACH FILLING

3 tbsp. (45 mL) butter

4 tbsp. (60 mL) finely chopped
   onions

¾ lb. (*340 g*) finely ground raw veal

10 oz. (*285 g*) pkg. frozen chopped
   spinach (defrosted, thoroughly
   squeezed & chopped again) OR
   ¾ lb. (*340 g*) fresh spinach,
   cooked, squeezed & chopped

½ cup (*125 mL*) freshly grated
   Parmesan cheese

pinch of ground nutmeg

3 eggs

salt to taste

pasta dough, see page 61

Ricotta & Parmesan Filling: In a large mixing bowl, combine the ricotta, Parmesan cheese, onion, egg yolks and salt. Carefully stir them together until they are well mixed. Set aside until you have rolled out the dough.

Veal & Spinach Filling: Melt the butter in a small skillet and cook the onions, stirring frequently, for 7 to 8 minutes, until they are soft and translucent, but not brown. Add the veal and cook, stirring constantly, until the veal loses its red color and any accumulating liquid in the pan cooks completely away. Transfer the entire contents of the skillet to a mixing bowl and stir in the chopped spinach, grated Parmesan cheese and a pinch of nutmeg. In a separate bowl, beat the eggs lightly and add them to the veal and spinach mixture. Taste and season with salt.

Divide the pasta dough into 4 pieces and roll out the first piece to make it as thin as possible. Cover the rolled pasta with a damp towel to prevent it drying out. Roll out the second piece of dough to a similar size and shape. Using the first sheet of rolled-out pasta as a sort of checkerboard, place a mound of about 1 tbsp. (15 mL) of the ricotta filling or the veal filling every 2" (5 cm) across and down the pasta. Dip a pastry brush or your index finger into a bowl of water and make vertical and horizontal lines in a checkerboard pattern on the sheet of pasta, between the mounds of filling.

Continued on the next page

RAVIOLI *(Continued)*

Be sure to use enough water to wet the lines evenly (the water will act as a bond to hold the finished ravioli together). Carefully spread the second sheet of rolled-out pasta on top of the first one, pressing down firmly around the filling and along the wetted lines.

With a ravioli cutter, a pastry wheel or a small, sharp knife, cut the pasta into squares along the wetted lines.

Separate the mounds of ravioli and set them aside on waxed paper. In the same fashion, roll out, fill and cut the 2 other portions of dough.

To cook, drop the ravioli into 6 to 8 quarts of rapidly boiling salted water. Stir gently with a wooden spoon to keep them from sticking to one another or to the bottom of the pot. Boil the ravioli for about 8 minutes, or until they are tender, then drain them thoroughly in a large sieve or colander.

Serve the ravioli with tomato sauce, see page 20, or add butter and freshly grated Parmesan cheese, and gently stir them immediately before serving.

Makes about 60

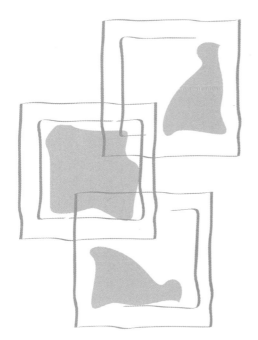

Pennette al Salmone

(Penne with Salmon Sauce)

Smoked salmon is not a traditional Italian ingredient, but it is becoming part of contemporary Italian cuisine. Once you taste this extraordinary sauce you'll know why!

1 tbsp. *(15 mL)* butter

2 chopped shallots

2 cups *(500 mL)* sliced fresh mushrooms

4 oz. *(125 g)* chopped smoked salmon

½ cup *(125 mL)* brandy

½ tsp. *(2 mL)* EACH salt & pepper

3 cups *(750 mL)* whipping cream (32% m.f.)

1 lb. *(500 g)* penne

1 tbsp. *(15 mL)* grated Parmesan cheese

Heat the butter in a frying pan. Add the shallots, mushrooms and salmon and sauté for 5 minutes.

Add the brandy and cook for 20 minutes. Add salt, pepper and whipping cream.

In a large pot of boiling, salted water, cook the penne for 10 minutes. Drain the penne and stir into the sauce. Sprinkle the cheese on top and serve.

Serves 6

Preparation Time: 10 minutes
Cooking Time: 20 minutes

PASTA CON TONNO E OLIVE

(PASTA WITH TUNA & OLIVES)

Rich in flavor, flaky and tender, tuna combines well with the distinctive flavors of ripe Italian olives and tomatoes in this traditional sauce.

2 tbsp. *(30 mL)* olive oil

2 garlic cloves, minced

28 oz. *(796 mL)* can tomatoes

½ tsp. *(2 mL)* EACH dried oregano, salt & pepper

¼ tsp. *(1 mL)* hot pepper flakes

1 lb. *(500 g)* bucatini*

1 cup *(250 mL)* medium, sliced, pitted black Italian olives

¼ cup *(60 mL)* chopped fresh parsley

2 x 6.5 oz. *(184 g)* cans solid light tuna, drained, flaked

*I*n a large saucepan, heat oil over medium heat. Add garlic and cook for 10 seconds, or until golden brown. Add tomatoes, oregano, salt, pepper and hot pepper flakes; bring to a boil. Reduce heat to medium-low and cook for 15 minutes.

Meanwhile, in a large pot of boiling, salted water, cook the pasta for 8 to 10 minutes, until al dente. Drain well.

Stir the olives into the sauce and cook for 2 minutes. Toss the pasta with the sauce, parsley and tuna. Serve immediately.

Serves 6

Preparation Time: 10 minutes
Cooking Time: 20 minutes

* Bucatini is a hollow pasta, just a bit thicker than spaghetti, that comes in long strands. A thicker version is called bucatoni.

Penne All'Arrabbiata

(Penne with Spicy Tomato Sauce)

Arrabbiata means "angry" in Italian. It is usually used for spicy tomato sauces with chilies. This sauce is very easy to prepare and you can add chilies to turn up the heat or lower it as you desire.

2 lbs. *(1 kg)* penne

½ cup *(125 mL)* olive oil

4 tbsp. *(60 mL)* crushed garlic

1 tsp. *(5 mL)* crushed chilies

3 ripe tomatoes, peeled & coarsely diced

salt & pepper to taste

½ cup *(125 mL)* grated Parmesan cheese

*I*n a large pot of boiling, salted water cook the pasta for 10 to 15 minutes, until al dente. Drain.

While pasta is cooking, heat the oil in a skillet over medium heat. Add garlic and chilies and cook until garlic is golden in color. Add tomatoes. Reduce heat and continue to cook for 10 to 15 minutes, stirring frequently.

Add the pasta to the frying pan and toss well. Season to taste with salt and pepper, adding a bit more oil if you like. Serve immediately with Parmesan cheese.

Serves 6

Preparation Time: **10 minutes**
Cooking Time: **15 minutes**

Pictured opposite.

Spaghetti Con Polpette

(Spaghetti with Meatballs)

For many North Americans, Spaghetti & Meatballs was their first taste of "real" Italian food. This traditional recipe is made with equal amounts of veal and pork. It is still a classic.

MEATBALLS

8 oz. (250 g) ground veal

8 oz. (250 g) ground pork

3 eggs

2 cups (500 mL) bread crumbs

3 garlic cloves, minced

salt & pepper to taste

½ cup (125 mL) vegetable oil

2 cups (500 mL) grated Parmesan cheese

19 oz. (540 mL) canned tomatoes

1 onion, chopped

1 medium green pepper, chopped

½ cup (125 mL) chopped parsley

1 lb. (500 g) spaghetti

Combine the veal, pork, eggs, bread crumbs, garlic, Parmesan cheese, salt and pepper in a large bowl. Make 1" (2.5 cm) round balls.

In a large skillet, heat oil on high but not to the smoking point. The oil must be hot or the meatballs will stick. Cook until the meatballs are brown on all sides, about 15 minutes.

Remove some of the excess oil and add the onion, peppers and parsley. Cook until the onion and peppers are soft; add the tomatoes and juice. Simmer over low heat for 1 hour.

In a large pot of boiling, salted water, cook the spaghetti for 7 to 8 minutes, until al dente. Place the cooked spaghetti in bowls and add the meatballs and sauce.

Serves 4

Preparation Time: 1 hour
Cooking Time: 1 ½ hour

Pictured opposite.

LINGUINE PESCATORE

(LINGUINE WITH FRESH SEAFOOD)

This inspired recipe combines a tempting array of seafood is a robust tomato garlic sauce.

SEAFOOD SAUCE

2 tbsp. *(30 mL)* olive oil

3 fresh garlic cloves, minced

2 tbsp. *(30 mL)* chopped fresh parsley

2 tbsp. *(30 mL)* dried oregano

24 mussels in shells

8 oz. *(250 g)* calamari*, cut into 1" *(2.5 cm)* circles

½ lb. *(250 g)* scallops

24 shrimp

½ lb. *(250 g)* baby clams in shells

½ cup *(125 mL)* dry white wine

1 quart *(1 L)* coarsely chopped tomatoes

salt & pepper to taste

1 lb. *(500 g)* linguine

Heat the oil in a large skillet. Add garlic and sauté for 1 minute. Add herbs and sauté until the aroma is released.

Clean all of the seafood and add to the herb/garlic mixture. Sauté for 5 minutes. Add wine, tomatoes, salt and pepper to taste. Cook for 15 minutes. Throw out all unopened mussels and clams.

Meanwhile, in a large pot of boiling, salted water, cook the linguine for 5 minutes, until al dente. Drain the pasta and add to the seafood. Combine thoroughly. Transfer to a large platter and serve at the table.

Serves 6

Preparation Time: 20 minutes
Cooking Time: 25 minutes

* See the note about cleaning calamari on page 34.

Scampi Alla Cardinale

(Prawns Cardinal Style)

Whipping cream and brandy, this luxurious tomato sauce with scampi would delight any cardinal.

2 lbs. *(1 kg)* scampi*

salt & pepper to taste

¼ lb. *(125 g)* butter

1 lb. *(500 g)* linguine

¼ cup *(60 mL)* brandy

1 cup *(250 mL)* whipping cream (32% m.f.)

2 cups *(500 mL)* tomato sauce, see page 20

Cut the scampi in half lengthwise and devein. Place in a shallow metal 8 x 10" (20 x 25 cm) baking dish and season with salt and pepper. Dot evenly with butter. Bake at 350°F (180°C) for 5 minutes.

Meanwhile, in a large pot of boiling salted water, cook linguine until al dente, 5 to 6 minutes.

Place the scampi dish on a burner over medium heat. Add the brandy, cream, and tomato sauce. Reduce heat and simmer until the sauce thickens. Pour over the cooked linguine.

Serves 4

Preparation Time: 10 minutes
Cooking Time: 15 minutes

* Scampi are Italian crustaceans that are similar to small lobsters (prawns). Called *langoustine* in French and *langostino* in Spanish, in North America large shrimp are sometimes called scampi.

Gamberetti Alla Portofino

(Shrimp with Tomato Mushroom Sauce)

Demi-glace adds a deep rich flavor that complements the earthy flavor of the mushrooms.

Shrimp, Tomato & Mushroom Sauce

½ cup *(125 mL)* olive oil

3 lbs *(1.5 kg)* shrimp, peeled, deveined

flour for coating

2 cups *(500 mL)* sliced mushrooms

3 garlic cloves, minced

½ cup *(125 mL)* green peas

1 cup *(250 mL)* white wine

2 cups *(500 mL)* tomato sauce, see page 20

1 cup *(250 mL)* demi-glace, see page 13

salt & pepper to taste

1 tbsp. *(15 mL)* chopped parsley

1 lb. *(500 g)* angel hair pasta

Heat the oil in a saucepan. Toss the shrimp in the flour and sauté for approximately 2 minutes.

Add the mushrooms, garlic, peas, wine, tomato sauce and demi-glace. Season and continue cooking for a few minutes. Add the parsley and stir.

In a large pot of boiling, salted water, cook the pasta for 3 to 4 minutes, until al dente. Pour the sauce over the cooked pasta.

Serves 6

Preparation Time: 30 minutes
Cooking Time: 10 minutes

Linguine Con Capesante

(Linguine with Scallops)

The delicate succulent flavor of scallops is enhanced by the perfect balance of this rich creamy sauce.

1 lb. (*500 g*) linguine noodles

CREAMY SCALLOP & MUSHROOM SAUCE

2 tbsp. (*30 mL*) olive oil

1 lb. (*500 g*) scallops

2 shallots, chopped

1 cup (*250 mL*) sliced mushrooms

2 garlic cloves, crushed

¼ cup (*60 mL*) white wine

1 quart (*1 L*) cream

1 tbsp. (*15 mL*) chopped fresh parsley

salt & pepper to taste

1 cup (*250 mL*) Parmesan cheese

*I*n a large pot of boiling, salted water, cook the linguine for 5 to 8 minutes, until al dente.

Meanwhile, in a large saucepan, heat the oil and sauté the scallops, shallots, mushrooms and garlic together for approximately 3 minutes. Add white wine, cream and parsley; reduce the liquid for an additional 5 minutes.

Drain the linguine and add to the sauce. Add salt and pepper to taste and stir in the Parmesan cheese. Cook until the sauce thickens. Serve immediately.

Serves 6

Preparation Time: 10 minutes
Cooking Time: 25 minutes

SPAGHETTI CARBONARA

(SPAGHETTI WITH HAM AND EGGS)

Perfect for brunch or a light supper, this traditional Roman dish is easy to prepare. The flavor is rich and the texture is creamy. Pancetta and cracked pepper add just the right sweet, salty, spicy note.

2 tbsp. *(30 mL)* olive oil

8 oz. *(250 g)* pancetta or bacon, diced

2 eggs

2 egg yolks

1 tbsp. *(15 mL)* cracked pepper

1 lb. *(500 g)* spaghetti

6 to 8 tbsp. *(90 to 120 mL)* Parmesan cheese, or to taste

*I*n a large pot of boiling, salted water, cook the spaghetti for 7 to 8 minutes, until al dente.

Meanwhile, in a skillet, heat the olive oil and sauté the bacon. Drain off excess fat. Add the spaghetti.

In a separate bowl, mix eggs and pepper together and add to the spaghetti. Keep the burner on medium heat and stir constantly while slowly adding the cheese. Add a small amount of water to make the sauce smooth.

Serves 4 to 6

Preparation Time: 5 minutes
Cooking Time: 15 minutes

Spaghetti Con Zucchini E Prosciutto

(Spaghetti with Zucchini & Ham)

Prosciutto means ham in Italian, but there is a profound flavor variation from prosciutto di Parma and North American ham. Prosciutto is made from pigs fed a special diet of chestnuts and/or the whey from Parmesan cheese. It is salt cured and air dried with a firm texture. The flavor is exceptional. Substitute ham if you cannot find prosciutto.

1 lb. (*500 g*) spaghetti

Zucchini & Prosciutto Sauce

2 cups (*500 mL*) stewed tomatoes

½ cup (*125 mL*)tomato paste

¾ cup (*175 mL*) prosciutto or cooked ham, slivered

1 medium zucchini, quartered lengthwise, thinly sliced

2 cups (*500 mL*) sliced mushrooms

½ cup (*125 mL*) milk

½ cup (*125 mL*) grated Parmesan cheese

In a large pot of boiling, salted water, cook the spaghetti for 7 to 8 minutes, until al dente. Drain.

Combine the tomatoes, tomato paste, prosciutto, zucchini and mushrooms in a saucepan. Bring just to a boil; reduce heat and simmer for 5 minutes.

Stir in the milk and ¼ cup (60 mL) of cheese; heat thoroughly. Serve over the cooked pasta. Sprinkle with remaining cheese.

Serves 4

Preparation Time: 10 minutes
Cooking Time: 20 minutes

LINGUINE CON PROSCIUTTO E PISELLI

(LINGUINE WITH HAM & PEAS)

Green peas add bright color and fresh flavor that contrasts well with the sweet saltiness of prosciutto.

1 lb. *(500 g)* linguine

5 oz. *(140 g)* prosciutto, very thinly sliced, chopped

2 tbsp. *(30 mL)* extra-virgin olive oil

3 tbsp. *(45 mL)* thinly sliced fresh garlic

½ cup *(125 mL)* shaved Parmesan cheese

2 tbsp. *(30 mL)* chopped fresh parsley

½ tsp. *(2 mL)* freshly grated black pepper

12 oz. *(340 g)* fresh peas or 10 oz. *(285 g)* pkg. frozen peas, steamed, drained

*I*n a large pot of boiling, salted water, cook the linguine for 5 minutes, until al dente. Drain

Heat a large skillet brushed with oil over medium heat. Add the prosciutto and cook for 2 minutes, or until lightly browned. Remove from the pan.

Add the oil and garlic and cook for 1 minute.

Combine the prosciutto, oil and garlic, pasta and remaining ingredients in a large bowl. Toss to coat and serve.

Serves 4 to 6

Preparation Time: 15 minutes
Cooking Time: 8 minutes

MAIN COURSES

*I*n my first cookbook, *The Fine Art of Italian Cooking,* I included many of the best known poultry, game and meat dishes from Molise, on the Adriatic coast of southern Italy. Here I have chosen a sampling of different recipes that are well known in the towns and provinces of Italy where they originated and have not yet become popular in North America. I have tried to choose specialties from as many of the regions and provinces as possible. Only the most distinguished chicken, lamb, beef, pork and veal dishes of Molise are featured in this book.

Frutti Di Mare

(Fish & Seafood)

*T*here are many rivers in Molise and a coastline borders its entire length, so both freshwater and ocean fish are plentiful. The fish is so good, in fact, that most of the time it is cooked very simply: grilled over a wood fire or on a spit; deep-fried with the lightest of coatings; poached and served with an uncooked herb sauce. But, of course, there are also dishes that are more complex, and I present some of those here.

*A*lthough it is difficult to match some varieties of fish, sweet shrimp or tiny clams that come from the Adriatico, substitutions can be made and satisfying results can be achieved.

Calamari Ripieni

(Stuffed Squid)

Squid is readily available and very popular in Italy and throughout the Mediterranean. The secret to cooking tender squid is DO NOT OVERCOOK.

1 ½ lbs. *(750 g)* whole calamari*

1 garlic clove, crushed

2 tbsp. *(30 mL)* chopped parsley

3 tbsp. *(45 mL)* bread crumbs

½ cup *(125 mL)* white wine

1 tbsp. *(15 mL)* olive oil

1 egg yolk

salt & pepper to taste

* See note on cleaning calamari on page 34.

Clean and peel the calamari; pull off the tentacles.

Chop the garlic, parsley and tentacles together. Add the bread crumbs, wine, olive oil, egg yolk, salt and pepper and mix well.

Stuff each calamari tube with the bread crumb mixture and close each end with a toothpick. Do not overstuff the squid or they may split while they are cooking. Place the stuffed calamari in a baking dish, rub with oil and season with salt and pepper.

Bake at 350°F (180°C) for 20 to 30 minutes.

Serves 4

Preparation Time: 1 hour
Cooking Time: 30 minutes

Funghi E Cape Sante Al Forno

(Baked Mushrooms and Scallops)

Sweet and mild flavored, scallops stay moist and tender in this recipe. As with other shellfish, it is important to NOT OVERCOOK them.

12 large mushroom caps

12 scallops

salt & pepper to taste

1 cup *(250 mL)* tomato sauce, see page 20

1 cup *(250 mL)* grated mozzarella cheese

In 2 escargot dishes, place 1 mushroom cap in each of the holes. Place 1 scallop on top of each mushroom. Season with salt and pepper. Pour tomato sauce over the scallops and cover with cheese.

Bake for 20 minutes at 400°F (200°C).

Serves 2

Preparation Time: 5 minutes
Cooking Time: 20 minutes

Cozze Alla Marinara*

(Mussels with Marinara Sauce)

Garlic and wine, subtly flavored with herbs, make an aromatic sauce for mussels. The anchovy adds a flavor fillip.

7 lbs. *(3.2 kg)* fresh mussels

½ cup *(125 mL)* olive oil

2 tsp. *(10 mL)* finely chopped fresh parsley

1 bay leaf

1 tsp. *(5 mL)* dried thyme

1 cup *(250 mL)* white wine

1 anchovy fillet in oil, finely chopped

2 garlic cloves, minced

salt & pepper to taste

Scrub the mussels thoroughly; remove the beards from the sides of the mussels and rinse several times. Discard any mussels that are open and will not close when pinched lightly.

In a large saucepan, heat the olive oil; add 1 tsp. (5 mL) parsley, the bay leaf, thyme and mussels. Pour in the wine and stir well. Cover and let cook over high heat. As soon as the mussels begin to open, in about 10 to 12 minutes, remove the saucepan from the heat. Discard the bay leaf and remove the mussels. Discard any unopened mussels.

Strain the liquid. Pour it back into the saucepan and return it to the heat. Add the parsley, anchovy, garlic, salt and pepper. Stir well. Reduce the heat and simmer until the sauce has thickened.

Place the mussels on a serving platter. Pour the sauce over and serve immediately.

Serves 6

Preparation Time: 5 minutes
Cooking Time: 10 minutes

* In North America, marinara sauces are spicy tomato sauces, seasoned with garlic, onions and oregano. In Italy, marinara sauces are more mild, focusing on the flavor of the seafood.

COZZE E VONGOLE LIVORNESE

(MUSSELS AND CLAMS LIVORNO STYLE)

Simple and sensational, this recipe allows the diner to enjoy the essential flavors of the mussels and clams.

1 lb. *(500 g)* mussels, cleaned, see page 98

1 lb. *(500 g)* clams, washed & cleaned

¼ cup *(60 mL)* olive oil

1 garlic clove, crushed

½ onion, diced

1 medium carrot, diced

salt & pepper to taste

pinch dried chili peppers

1 cup *(250 mL)* white wine

Prepare the mussels and clams.

In a large pot, heat the oil and sauté the garlic, onions and carrots. Add mussels, clams, salt and pepper. Add the chili peppers and wine and cover. Cook for about 10 minutes and serve.

Discard any unopened mussels or clams.

Serves 4

Preparation Time: 5 minutes
Cooking Time: 20 minutes

NOTE: Livorno (Leghorn), in Tuscany, on the Ligurian Sea, is famous for its Cacciucco alla Livornese (Seafood Stew) which rivals the renowned Bouillabaisse of Marseilles.

VONGOLE AL FORNO

(BAKED CLAMS)

Savour the smoky flavor of bacon and the tang of garlic with these delicious tomato-sauced clams.

2 lbs. *(1 kg)* fresh clams, washed & cleaned

2 tbsp. *(30 mL)* olive oil

1 chopped onion

1 garlic clove, crushed

½ cup *(125 mL)* chopped, lightly smoked bacon

2 tbsp. *(30 mL)* chopped parsley

2 cups *(500 mL)* tomato sauce, see page 20

½ cup *(125 mL)* Parmesan cheese

*P*repare the clams.

In a large pot, heat the oil and sauté the onions, garlic and bacon; add the clams and parsley and cook for 5 to 6 minutes. Discard any clams that do not open.

Pour the contents of the pot into a baking dish and top with tomato sauce. Sprinkle with Parmesan cheese.

Bake at 350°F (180°C) for 15 minutes.

Serves 6

Preparation Time: 10 minutes
Cooking Time: 25 minutes

Vongole Mediterranio

(Baked Clams & Rice with Saffron)

Crush the saffron threads just before adding them to the dish. The pungent aroma of saffron adds to the pleasure of cooking with it. Saffron and seafood are an irresistable combination.

2 lbs. *(1 kg)* fresh clams, washed & cleaned

¼ cup *(60 mL)* dry white wine

½ tsp. *(2 mL)* finely chopped garlic

3 tbsp. *(45 mL)* + 2 tbsp. *(30 mL)* butter

½ medium onion, peeled, finely chopped

2 cups *(500 mL)* long-grain white rice

½ tsp. *(2 mL)* saffron threads*

3 cups *(750 mL)* chicken stock

2 tbsp. *(30 mL)* washed, chopped scallions

Put the clams in a large pot with the wine and garlic. Cover the pot and steam for 5 to 6 minutes until the clams open. Discard any that do not open. Drain the clams, reserving the liquid.

Remove the clams from the shells, leaving some in shells for garnish. Set clams aside. Strain the clam liquid into a bowl through a sieve lined with a linen cloth. Set aside.

Melt 3 tbsp. (45 mL) of butter in an ovenproof 2-quart (2 L) casserole. Sauté the onions for 2 to 3 minutes. Add rice and saffron and gently stir to coat with butter. Add the chicken stock and clam liquid and bring to a boil. Stir once, reduce the heat and cover the casserole.

Place the casserole in the oven and bake at 300°F (150°C) for 15 minutes. Remove from the oven and uncover. Add the clams and 2 tbsp. (30 mL) of butter; gently mix together. Re-cover and bake for 5 to 7 minutes.

Remove the casserole from the oven. Uncover and sprinkle with scallions. Garnish with reserved clams in shells and serve immediately.

Serves 4

Preparation Time: **20 minutes**
Cooking Time: **30 minutes**

* See the saffron note on page 181.

Aragosta Al Brandy

(Lobster with Brandy Sauce)

A creamy brandy sauce with lobster is gilding the lily, but this is a fabulous dish for a very special occasion.

4 lobsters*, about 1 lb. (*500 g*) each, cooked

salt & pepper to taste

½ cup (*125 mL*) butter

1 garlic clove, minced

½ cup (*125 mL*) brandy

1 quart (1 L) whipping cream (32% m.f.)

1 tsp. (*5 mL*) fresh parsley, chopped fine

Wash the lobsters several times. Cut off the claws and crack the claw shells. Split each lobster in half lengthwise. Remove the head sac and intestines of each lobster. (The green/grey tomalley [liver] and red coral [eggs] are edible and flavorful.) Season lobster and claws with salt and pepper.

In a large skillet melt butter and add the lobster, cook for 10 minutes on medium heat. Add the garlic, brandy, cream and cook for an additional 5 minutes. Remove the lobsters and claws and keep warm. Continue cooking the sauce for about 15 minutes. Season the sauce with more salt and pepper and add the parsley. Stir well.

When ready to serve, pour the sauce over the lobsters and the claws. Serve with rice or pasta. Serve immediately.

Serves 4

Preparation Time: **10 minutes**
Cooking Time: **30 minutes**

Pictured opposite.

* Live lobsters should be vigorous when you buy them, moving their claws and flipping their curled tails.

To cook live lobsters, bring a large pot of water to a boil (at least 2 quarts (2 L) of water per 1 lb. (500 g) lobster). Add lobsters, do not crowd them; cover the pot and parboil for about 3 minutes per pound (500 g). The lobsters will have started to turn red and will have stopped moving. Proceed as indicated in the recipe. To fully cook lobsters, boil for 10 minutes per pound (500 g).

When buying whole, cooked lobsters, check to make sure that the tail is curled. This indicates that it was alive when it was cooked.

Christmas Eve

Antipasto Frutti Di Mare (Cold Seafood Appetizer), Page 33

Dinner

ARAGOSTA DI PESARO

(LOBSTER IN LEMON SAUCE)

Often the simple things are the best, wonderful ingredients simply prepared. Lemon and wine enhance the natural lobster flavor in this recipe.

4 lobster tails

½ cup *(125 mL)* white wine

½ cup *(125 mL)* butter

1 lemon

2 garlic cloves, minced

1 tsp. *(5 mL)* chopped parsley

salt & pepper to taste

Cut the lobster tails lengthwise down the back and peel out the meat. Rest the meat on the shell. Place on a baking sheet and bake at 350°F (180°C) for 10 to 20 minutes.

In a small saucepan, heat wine, butter, lemon, garlic, parsley, salt and pepper. Bring to a boil. The sauce should thicken, if it doesn't, add a little beurre manier, see page 14.

To serve, place the lobster on a platter and pour the sauce over it.

Serves 4

Preparation Time: 10 minutes
Cooking Time: 10 to 20 minutes

Ostriche alla Medici

(Baked Oysters and Spinach served with Walnut Sauce)

Spinach is associated with Florentine cuisine, and the Medici family once ruled Florence and were noted patrons of the arts during the Italian Rennaissance. This seductive oyster dish is both aristocratic and elegant – a fitting tribute.

1 ½ lbs. (*750 g*) fresh oysters, shucked, reserving the bottom shells

Walnut Sauce

1 cup (*250 mL*) white wine

¼ cup (*60 mL*) finely chopped fresh walnuts

3 egg yolks

1 tsp. (*5 mL*) freshly squeezed lemon juice

salt & pepper to taste

4-6 bunches fresh spinach, washed and stemmed

2 tbsp. (*30 mL*) pernod

2 tbsp. (*30 mL*) finely chopped onion

½ tsp. (*2 mL*) finely chopped garlic

salt & pepper to taste

pinch of ground nutmeg

½ lemon, juice of

2 tbsp. (*30 mL*) finely chopped fresh walnuts

2 tbsp. (*30 mL*) finely chopped fresh parsley

*P*ut the oyster meat in a bowl and set aside. Put bottoms of oyster shells in a pot of boiling water for 1 minute. Remove, pat dry, set aside.

*S*auce: Heat the wine in a small saucepan. Stir in the walnuts. Remove from the heat and blend in egg yolks. Stir in the lemon juice. Season with salt and pepper.

Cook the spinach in a pot containing pernod, onion, garlic, salt, pepper and nutmeg for 1 minute, until the spinach has just wilted. Drain spinach and chop coarsely. Put 1 tbsp. (15 mL) of spinach in the center of each oyster shell and set aside.

Blanch the oyster meat in a pot of boiling water for 1 minute; drain. Put the oysters on top of the spinach. Spoon the walnut sauce over the oysters to cover. Put the shells on a baking tray. Put in oven and bake at 400°F (200°C) for 5 to 7 minutes. Remove from oven and put shells on individual plates, 5 to 6 per plate. Sprinkle with lemon juice, walnuts and parsley. Serve immediately.

Serves 4

Preparation Time: 30 minutes
Cooking Time: 10-12 minutes

Spiedini Di Scampi

(Skewered Scampi)

Butter-baked scampi are sweet and succulent, the added tang and saltiness of prosciutto makes a great combination.

2 ½ lbs. *(1.25 kg)* scampi*, peeled and cleaned

3 thick slices of prosciutto, cubed

salt & pepper to taste

¼ cup *(60 mL)* softened butter

lemon wedges

Cut the scampi in half lengthwise, then thread the scampi onto metal skewers, alternating with cubed prosciutto. Sprinkle with salt and pepper, then brush with butter.

Place the skewers in a non-stick roasting pan. Place the roasting pan in the oven and bake at 400°F (200°C) for 15 minutes. Baste with pan juices.

When done, remove the scampi from the skewers and serve garnished with lemon wedges.

Serves 4 to 6

Preparation Time: **20 minutes**
Cooking Time: **10 minutes**

* If scampi are not available use large shrimp. See the scampi note on page 99.

GAMBERI ALLA PROVINCIALE

(SHRIMP WITH LEMON & GARLIC)

Garlic, lemon, shrimp and olive oil, indulge yourself in the sunny flavors of this quickly prepared country dish.

flour

salt & pepper to taste

8 large shrimp, shelled and deveined

2 tbsp. *(30 mL)* olive oil

1 tsp. *(5 mL)* minced parsley

2 garlic cloves, minced

¼ cup *(60 mL)* white wine

2 tbsp. *(30 mL)* butter

½ lemon, juice of

*I*n a shallow dish, combine a little flour with some salt and pepper and lightly roll the shrimp in the flour. Shake to remove excess flour.

In a skillet, heat the oil over high heat and sauté the shrimp about 1 minute per side, until just pink but not brown. Remove the pan from the heat and drain off excess oil.

Add the remaining ingredients to the pan and return to medium-high heat, allowing the sauce to boil. Swirl the pan occasionally to combine ingredients. Bring to a simmer and cook about 1 minute in total. Sprinkle with freshly ground pepper. Serve with rice or pasta if desired.

Serves 1

Preparation Time: 10 minutes
Cooking Time: 5 minutes

GAMBERI AL VINO BIANCO

(SHRIMP WITH WHITE WINE)

Throughout North America, shrimp is the favorite shellfish. This recipe adds the classic flavors of Italian cuisine – it's a winning combination.

1 tbsp. *(15 mL)* butter

¼ cup *(60 mL)* oil

1 medium onion, finely diced

2 stalks celery, finely chopped

1 medium carrot, finely chopped

3 ½ lbs. *(1.75 kg)* large shrimp, peeled, deveined

½ tsp. *(2 mL)* dried oregano

½ tsp. *(2 mL)* dried thyme

salt & pepper to taste

1 ½ cups *(375 mL)* dry white wine

*I*n a large skillet, heat the butter and oil; sauté the onion, celery, and carrot over medium heat for about 5 minutes.

Add the shrimp and stir well. Cook for another 5 minutes. Add oregano, thyme, salt and pepper and stir well. Pour wine over shrimp and continue cooking over medium heat for about 15 minutes, stir occasionally.

Serves 6

Preparation Time: 30 minutes
Cooking Time: 20 minutes

Trotelle alla Mignaia con Gamberetti

(Pan-Fried Fillet of Trout with Shrimp)

Crisp golden pan-fried trout is topped with parsley-flecked sautéed shrimp, an irresistible combination.

4, 8-10 oz. *(250-285 g)* whole fresh trout, filleted, each in 2 halves, head, tail, fins removed

salt & white pepper to taste

2 ½ lemons, juice of

dash of Worcestershire sauce

flour (to dust)

6 tbsp. *(90 mL)* olive oil

¼ cup *(60 mL)* + 3 tbsp. *(45 mL)* butter

¼ lb. *(125 g)* fresh shrimp

1 ½ tbsp. *(7 mL)* finely chopped fresh parsley

Rinse the trout fillets under cold water and pat dry with paper towels. Season with salt and pepper. Sprinkle with the juice of 1 lemon and Worcestershire sauce. Dust with flour.

Fry the fillets in all of the oil and 3 tbsp. (45 mL) butter in a skillet for 1 to 2 minutes per side. Remove and put skin-side down on a platter. Keep platter warm. Drain off oil.

Add ¼ cup (60 mL) butter to the skillet and sauté the shrimp for 1 minute. Add the rest of the lemon juice to the skillet and blend in. Sprinkle with parsley. Season with salt and pepper.

Spoon the shrimp sauce over the trout fillets and serve immediately.

Serves 4

Preparation Time: 15 minutes
Cooking Time: 5 minutes

TROTELLE AL BLEU

(POACHED TROUT)

In the traditional Truite au Bleu, freshly killed trout are plunged into boiling court-bouillon and the skin turns blue. For this effect the skin of the fish must not be washed – the trout's protective coating is what turns blue. This trout, poached is a vinegar/water bouillon, has a fresh flavor and a lovely lemon butter sauce.

4 fresh trout

4 quarts *(4 L)* water

salt to taste

3 cups *(750 mL)* white vinegar

½ cup *(125 mL)* butter

1 lemon, juice of

Clean the trout thoroughly.

In a large pot bring salted water to a boil and add the vinegar and trout. Reduce the heat and simmer for 10 minutes. Drain.

In a small saucepan, melt the butter and the lemon juice; stir. Pour the sauce over the trout.

Serves 4

Preparation Time: 5 minutes
Cooking Time: 15 minutes

Salmone Al Funghi

(Salmon with Mushrooms)

The early Romans prized mushrooms and used them in a wide variety of recipes. The rich flavors of salmon and mushrooms blend beautifully in this very easy-to-prepare dish.

flour

4, 6 oz. *(170 g)* fresh salmon steaks

salt & pepper to taste

1 cup *(250 mL)* butter

3 cups *(750 mL)* thickly sliced fresh mushrooms

1 lemon, juice of

Flour the salmon and season with salt and pepper. In an ovenproof skillet, fry the salmon in butter for 5 minutes over high heat; add the mushrooms.

Turn the salmon over and place the skillet in a 400°F (200°C) oven for about 5 to 10 minutes, or until you can pull out the center bone. Remove the salmon from the oven and sprinkle with lemon juice.

Serves 4

Preparation Time: 5 minutes
Cooking Time: 15 minutes

Petti Di Pollo Al Vino Bianco

(Chicken in White Wine)

Rosemary and garlic perfume the air when this tender chicken is served in a white wine sauce.

½ cup (125 mL) olive oil

flour

6 boneless chicken breasts, 12 halves

4 garlic cloves, minced

1 tsp. (5 mL) dried rosemary

1 cup (250 mL) white wine

2 cups (500 mL) chicken broth

1 tbsp. (15 mL) minced parsley

½ cup (125 mL) beurre manié, see page 14

Heat the oil in a large skillet. Flour the chicken and sauté until done, about 15 to 18 minutes.

Drain off the oil. Add the garlic and rosemary. Deglaze the pan with wine and broth. Add the parsley. Bring to a boil and add beurre manié stirring and cooking until the sauce thickens slightly.

Serves 6

Preparation Time: 10 minutes
Cooking Time: 20 minutes

Pollo Alle Mandorle

(Chicken with Almonds)

Marsala and almonds add smoky, nutty subtle flavor to this chicken dish.

½ cup *(125 mL)* olive oil

flour

6 boneless chicken breasts, 12 halves

1 ½ cups *(375 mL)* sliced almonds, toasted

1 cup *(250 mL)* Marsala*

2 cups *(500 mL)* demi-glace, see page 13

1 cup *(250 mL)* water

salt & pepper to taste

Heat the oil in a large skillet and dredge the chicken in flour. Fry the chicken breasts on each side for approximately 3 minutes per side.

Drain off the oil. Add the almonds and Marsala. Then add the demi-glace and water. Lower the heat and reduce the sauce until it thickens slightly. Add salt and pepper to taste.

Serves 6

Preparation Time: 10 minutes
Cooking Time: 20 minutes

*Marsala is a fortified wine made in Sicily. Famous for its smoky richness, it comes in sweet (*dolce*), semisweet (*semisecco*) and dry (*secco*) versions. The sweet and semisweet are usually served as dessert wines.

Pollo Ai Funghi Freschi

(Chicken with Fresh Mushrooms)

Fresh mushrooms and tomatoes create a colorful sauce for this hearty, satisfying recipe.

¼ cup *(60 mL)* olive oil

3 lb. *(1.5 kg)* chicken, cut in pieces

1 tbsp. *(15 mL)* finely chopped parsley

1 garlic clove, minced

salt to taste

2 cups *(500 mL)* thickly sliced fresh mushrooms

¾ lb. *(340 g)* ripe tomatoes, peeled, diced

3-4 tbsp. *(45-60 mL)* chicken broth

*I*n a large skillet, heat the oil over high heat. Add the chicken pieces and brown on all sides. Add the parsley, garlic, and salt. Stir well.

Reduce the heat and add the mushrooms; cook for 10 minutes.

Add the tomatoes and chicken broth. Continue cooking for another 30 minutes, or until the chicken is done, stirring frequently.

Serves 4

Preparation Time: 20 minutes
Cooking Time: 45 minutes

Pollo Alla Romana

(Chicken Roman Style)

Slowly simmered, this chicken is tender and the aroma is robust and tantalizing.

4 lb. *(2 kg)* frying chicken

1 cup *(250 mL)* olive oil

flour

1 cup *(250 mL)* sliced mushrooms

1 medium onion, sliced

1 red pepper, sliced

1 green pepper, sliced

3 garlic cloves, minced

1 tbsp. *(15 mL)* chopped rosemary

1 quart (1 L) chopped canned
  tomatoes

salt & pepper to taste

1 tsp. *(5 mL)* chopped parsley

Cut the chicken into 8 pieces. Heat the oil in a large skillet. Flour the chicken and fry it until it is browned.

Put the chicken in a large pot with the mushrooms, onions, peppers, garlic and rosemary. Add the tomatoes, cover and simmer for 1 hour.

Add salt, pepper and parsley. Serve over pasta.

Serves 4

Preparation Time: 20 minutes
Cooking Time: 1 hour

Pollo Alla Cacciatora

(Chicken Hunter-Style)

Hunter-style used to mean food prepared in the field, with ingredients readily available or transportable. This hunter-style chicken recipe is bursting with flavor – anchovies, garlic, herbs and wine.

2 anchovy fillets in oil

2 garlic cloves, minced

6 sprigs fresh parsley

1 tsp. *(5 mL)* dried rosemary

4 lb. *(2 kg)* chicken

salt and pepper to taste

½ cup *(125 mL)* flour

½ cup *(125 mL)* olive oil

1 cup *(250 mL)* dry white wine

2 cups *(500 mL)* chicken broth, see page 12

½ cup *(125 mL)* beurre manié, see page 14

*F*inely chop the anchovy, garlic, parsley, rosemary, and mix well. Set aside.

Cut up the chicken and season with salt and pepper. Flour the chicken and shake off any excess flour.

In a large skillet, heat the oil and brown the chicken pieces on all sides over medium heat. Remove the skillet from the heat and discard any excess oil, leaving the chicken pieces in the skillet.

Return the pan to the heat and add the anchovy mixture. Stir well. Pour the wine over the chicken and continue cooking on low heat. Add the chicken broth and bring to a boil. Stir in beurre manié until smooth. Continue cooking for 30 minutes.

Serves 6

Preparation Time: **20 minutes**
Cooking Time: **45 minutes**

STUFFED CHICKEN LEGS

Parmesan and prosciutto add full-bodied flavor to this simple yet impressive dish.

4 chicken legs

2 eggs

2 garlic cloves, minced

1 medium onion

1 ²⁄₃ cup *(400 mL)* grated Parmesan

¹⁄₂ cup *(125 mL)* bread crumbs

3 ¹⁄₂ oz. *(100 g)* proscuitto, minced

2 tbsp. *(30 mL)* white vinegar

salt & pepper to taste

¹⁄₂ cup *(125 mL)* extra-virgin olive oil

¹⁄₂ cup *(125 mL)* white wine

*B*one the chicken legs.

To make the stuffing, mix all of the remaining ingredients together, except the wine.

Put the stuffing into the boned chicken legs and shape into cylinders. Place in a shallow baking pan.

Bake at 350°F (180°C) for 30 minutes. After 15 minutes of cooking add the white wine. Serve with vegetables or pasta.

Serves 4

Preparation Time: 30 to 45 minutes
Cooking Time: 30 minutes

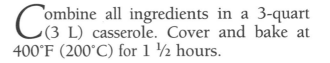

POLLO IN UMIDO

(STEWED CHICKEN LEGS)

Very easy, economical and very good – one-pot recipes are perfect for busy families.

8 chicken legs

4 medium potatoes, sliced ½" (1.5 cm) thick

1 green pepper, sliced

1 red pepper, sliced

4 garlic cloves, minced

1 tsp. *(5 mL)* oregano

1 tbsp. *(15 mL)* chopped parsley

2 quarts *(2 L)* canned tomatoes, chopped

2 cups *(500 mL)* chicken broth, see page 12, or water

salt & pepper to taste

Combine all ingredients in a 3-quart (3 L) casserole. Cover and bake at 400°F (200°C) for 1 ½ hours.

Serves 4

Preparation Time: 20 minutes
Cooking Time: 1 ½ - 2 hours

Petti Di Pollo Alla Milanese

(Breaded Chicken Milan Style)

This crispy pan-fried chicken has a delicate golden crust and is tender and juicy inside.

4 boneless chicken breasts

2 eggs, slightly beaten

½ cup (125 mL) milk

½ cup (125 mL) flour

2 cups (500 mL) bread crumbs

½ cup (125 mL) olive oil

Pound the chicken breasts until they are very thin and 2 to 3 times larger than the original size.

In a shallow pan, beat together the eggs and milk. Dredge the chicken in the flour, then dip it in the egg mixture and then in the bread crumbs.

Heat the oil in a large skillet, over medium-high heat, and fry the chicken until golden brown.

Serves 4

Preparation Time: 15 minutes
Cooking Time: 10 minutes

Pollastrella Alla Diavala

(Cornish Hen with Lemon)

Crisp skin and a light dressing of butter and lemon, these Cornish hens are so simple to prepare and so good.

2 Cornish hens, cut in half
  lengthwise

salt & pepper to taste

¼ cup (60 mL) vegetable oil

1 tbsp. (15 mL) butter

2 lemons, juice of

Season the Cornish hens with salt and pepper.

Heat the oil in a large ovenproof skillet until it smokes. Lay the hens in the skillet skin-side down. Place in the oven and bake at 400°F (200°C) for 20 to 40 minutes, or until done. Remove the hens from the oven. Drain off excess fat. Add butter and lemon juice.

Serves 4

Preparation Time: 5 minutes
Cooking Time: 20 to 40 minutes

POLLO RIPIENO

(STUFFED CORNISH HEN)

Basil, Parmesan and garlic add gusto to this dressing.

PARMESAN BASIL STUFFING

½ green pepper, finely diced

1 tbsp. *(15 mL)* crushed garlic cloves

2 eggs

2 basil leaves, chopped

1 cup *(250 mL)* bread crumbs

1 cup *(250 mL)* Parmesan cheese

salt & pepper to taste

1 Cornish hen

1 carrot, finely diced

1 celery stalk, finely diced

2 cups *(500 mL)* white wine

Combine the stuffing ingredients in a large bowl until well blended and firm.

Stuff the hen. Roast the hen in a baking pan at 400°F (200°C) for 30 minutes.

Add the carrot, celery and wine to the bottom of the pan and continue cooking for another 30 minutes.

Remove the hen from the oven and split it in half. Pour the sauce over the hen.

Serves 2

Preparation Time: 15 minutes
Cooking Time: 1 hour

Arrosto Di Quaglie

(Roasted Quails)

This tomato sauce is a hearty blend of flavors, with added bacon, shallots and white wine.

8 quails

salt & pepper to taste

4 slices of bacon, diced

4 shallots, diced

½ cup (125 mL) white wine

2 cups (500 mL) tomato sauce, see page 20

Season the quails with salt and pepper and place in a shallow baking dish. Bake at 400°F (200°C) for 20 minutes.

Remove the quails from the pan and place the pan over high heat, adding the bacon and shallots. Cook for 5 minutes. Pour off any fat and add the wine and tomato sauce.

Place the quails back into the pan and cook for another 5 minutes. Serve.

Serves 4

Preparation Time: 10 minutes
Cooking Time: 45 minutes

FAGIANI CON PORCINI

(PHEASANT WITH PORCINI SAUCE)

Pheasant has a lovely, very slight gamy flavor. The Barolo and porcini add a perfect balance of flavors.

1 oz. *(25 g)* dried porcini* mushrooms

½ cup *(125 mL)* hot water

2 boneless pheasant breasts**

flour

⅓ cup *(75 mL)* vegetable oil

1 shallot diced

½ cup *(125 mL)* Barolo wine***

1 cup *(250 mL)* demi-glace, see page 13

salt & pepper to taste

Soak the porcini in a the hot water.

Dredge the pheasant in flour.

Heat the oil in a large skillet. Add the pheasant and brown each side for 2 minutes. Drain off the grease and place the skillet in a 350°F (180°C) oven for 10 minutes.

Remove the breasts; add shallots and mushrooms to the skillet and place over medium heat. Add the wine and the juice from the mushrooms. Add the demi-glace; reduce the heat and simmer until thickened. Season the sauce with salt and pepper and pour it over the breasts.

Serves 2

Preparation Time: 10 minutes
Cooking Time: 20 minutes

* Porcini mushrooms (cèpes) are pale brown and have a meaty, smooth texture, an earthy flavor and pungent aroma. Dried mushrooms should be pale brown and not crumbly. Fresh porcini mushrooms are not often available in North America.

** Wild game should always be well cooked.

*** Barolo wine is robust, full-bodied, with a sensuous aroma. It is from the Piedmont region of Italy.

WILD DUCK ANTONIETTA

The robust flavor of wild duck is enhanced with a crunchy aromatic thyme coating.

1 medium duck

dash garlic salt

2-3 sprigs fresh thyme, or ¼ tsp.
  (1 mL) powdered

flour

salt & pepper to taste

2 cups *(500 mL)* vegetable oil

Cut the duck into 4 to 6 parts. Generously sprinkle garlic salt, thyme, salt and pepper over the duck pieces. Dip the duck into the flour.

In a 10" (25 cm) skillet, heat the vegetable oil to 365°F (185°C). Deep-fry the duck pieces for 10 to 15 minutes, depending on how you like your duck. If you use fresh thyme, add 2 or 3 sprigs after the duck has been frying for about 5 minutes, turn once.

The perfect accompaniment with duck prepared in this manner is a good green salad with olive oil and vinegar dressing.

Serves 2 to 4

Preparation Time: 1 hour
Cooking Time: 10 to 15 minutes

ABBACCHIO ALLA TOSCANA

(RACK OF LAMB)

Mild, tender and sweet, lamb is best served rare or medium rare. Because of the high proportion of bone to meat, these servings of 1 rack per person are generous but not too much. The flavor is fabulous.

4 racks of lamb*, 1 ¼ to 1 ½ lbs. (625 to 750 g) each

1 tsp. (5 mL) butter

4 shallots, chopped

1 tsp. (5 mL) *dried* rosemary

2 garlic cloves, minced

1 tsp. (5 mL) cracked pepper

1 cup (250 mL) red wine

1 cup (250 mL) demi-glace, see page 13

salt & pepper to taste

Sear the lamb in a heavy saucepan over high heat, until browned.

Roast the lamb at 350°F (180°C) until desired doneness is reached. Test with a meat thermometer 125°F (52°C) for rare, 130 to 135°F (54 to 57°C) for medium rare, about 20 to 30 minutes.

Meanwhile, in a small pot, melt the butter and add the shallots, rosemary, garlic and pepper. Sauté for 2 to 3 minutes and add the wine and demi-glace. Bring to a boil and reduce to a sauce consistency. Add salt and pepper and strain.

Remove the lamb from oven and let it rest for 5 to 10 minutes before cutting into single or double chops. Place the lamb on a platter and pour the sauce over.

Serves 4, 1 rack each

Preparation Time: 10 minutes
Cooking Time: 20 to 30 minutes

* A rack of lamb is the rib section of the lamb. It can be left whole, 7 to 8 ribs, or cut into individual or double chops.

Pictured on page 136.

NOTE: The racks of lamb should have the backbone (chine bone) removed to allow cutting the racks into separate chops. Trim off the heavy outer fat layer, if necessary, leaving only a thin layer of fat over the centre nugget of meat.

Cosciotto D'Agnello Arrosto

(Roasted Leg of Lamb)

Leg of lamb is a tender, delicately flavored cut. Roasting with garlic and rosemary brings out the best natural flavors.

3 lb. leg of lamb*

2 garlic cloves, minced

1 tsp. *(5 mL)* dried rosemary

salt & pepper to taste

1 cup (250 mL) olive oil

1 cup *(250 mL)* white wine

With a knife, cut slits about 1" (2.5 cm) long and ¼" (1 cm) deep into the leg of lamb. Lightly press garlic and rosemary into the slits and season with salt and pepper.

Place the leg of lamb in a roasting pan and pour the oil over it. Roast at 400°F (200°C) for about 30 minutes. Baste occasionally with pan juices.

Pour the wine over the lamb and continue roasting for another 30 minutes. Turn frequently and continue basting.

When ready to serve, place the leg of lamb on a platter and pour the juices over.

Serves 6 to 8

Preparation Time: **10 minutes**
Cooking Time: **1 hour**

* Lamb has a parchment-like white membrane (the fell) which must be removed before cooking. If the butcher has not removed the fell, cut it away from the meat. Also trim away most of the fat which may have a strong tallow flavor that can overpower the mild sweet flavor of the lamb. Lamb is best served rare (125°F/52°C) or medium rare (130 to 135°F/54 to 57°C). Test with a meat thermometer.

Agnello Alla Cacciatora

(Hunter's Lamb)

Rosemary and garlic are classic flavor accompaniments to lamb. This robust dish has the added enhancement of anchovies and white wine.

2 anchovy fillets (in oil)

2 garlic cloves

1 tsp. *(5 mL)* dried rosemary

6 parsley sprigs

4 lbs. *(2 kg)* lamb, cut into bite-sized pieces

salt & pepper to taste

½ cup *(125 mL)* flour

½ cup *(125 mL)* olive oil

1 cup *(250 mL)* white wine

2 cups *(500 mL)* chicken broth

beurre manié, see page 14

Finely chop the anchovy, garlic, rosemary, and parsley and mix well. Set aside.

Season the lamb with salt and pepper. Dredge the lamb in flour and shake off the excess.

In a large skillet, heat the oil and add the lamb. Brown on all sides over medium heat. Remove the skillet from the heat and discard the oil, leaving the lamb in the skillet.

Return the skillet to the heat and add the anchovy mixture. Stir well. Pour the wine over the lamb and continue cooking over low heat. Add the chicken broth; stir and reduce heat.

Stir in beurre manié to thicken and continue cooking for 30 minutes.

Serves 4 to 6

Preparation Time: 20 minutes
Cooking Time: 1 hour

COTOLETTE D'AGNELLO ALLA MILANESE

(BREADED LAMB CHOPS)

A crisp golden coating on very tender lamb chops, this recipe is very fast and very easy.

6 boneless lamb chops

salt & pepper to taste

½ cup *(125 mL)* flour

1 egg, beaten

2 cups *(500 mL)* bread crumbs

1 tbsp. *(15 mL)* butter

¼ cup *(60 mL)* olive oil

*P*ound the lamb chops firmly with a flat-surfaced mallet until each chop is 2 to 3 times larger than the original size.

Season with salt and pepper. Coat each chop with flour and shake off excess flour. Dip chops into egg, then coat well with bread crumbs.

In a large skillet heat butter and oil. Add the lamb chops and sauté over medium heat until golden brown, about 10 to 15 minutes.

Serve immediately with vegetables or pasta.

Serves 6

Preparation Time: 20 minutes
Cooking Time: 10 to 15 minutes

Piccata Al Limone

(Veal Scaloppini in Lemon Sauce)

For the most tender veal scaloppini buy the palest veal. These delicious scaloppini should melt in your mouth.

12 veal scaloppine, pounded

salt & pepper to taste

½ cup (125 mL) flour

½ cup (125 mL) oil

3 tbsp. (45 mL) butter

1 cup (250 mL) dry white wine

5 sprigs parsley, chopped finely

2 cups (500 mL) chicken broth, see page 12

1 lemon, juice of

1 tbsp. (15 mL) beurre manié, see page 14

*P*ound each piece of veal firmly with a flat-surfaced mallet until each piece is 2 to 3 times larger in size.

Season with salt and pepper. Lightly flour and shake off excess.

In a large heavy skillet heat the oil and 1 tbsp. (15 mL) butter over high heat; add the veal scaloppine. Cook each side for 2 minutes. Discard the oil and leave the veal in the skillet.

Add the wine, parsley, broth and lemon juice. Stir until blended. Lower the heat and reduce the sauce further. Stir in the beurre manié to thicken. Simmer for about 5 minutes. Remove from the heat.

Place the veal on individual plates and pour the sauce over. Serve with vegetables.

Serves 4 to 6

Preparation Time: 30 minutes
Cooking Time: 15 minutes

Bracioline Alla Panna Con Funghi

(Veal Scaloppini with Mushrooms and Cream Sauce)

Mushrooms and cream seem to have a natural affinity. This luscious dish is pure luxury.

2 lbs. (*1 kg*) white veal, trim away fat & membrane

salt & pepper to taste

½ cup (*125 mL*) flour

¼ cup (*60 mL*) oil

2 tbsp. (*30 mL*) butter

1 cup (*250 mL*) thickly sliced fresh mushrooms

½ cup (*125 mL*) dry white wine

1½ cups (*375 mL*) whipping cream (32% m.f.)

Cut the veal into 12 slices. Pound each piece of veal, using a flat-surfaced mallet, until each piece is 3 times larger in size.

Season each veal scaloppini with salt and pepper. Flour both sides and shake off excess.

In a large skillet, heat the oil and butter over medium heat. Add veal scaloppini and cook each side for about 2 minutes. Add the mushrooms and cook for 5 minutes.

Discard the oil, leaving the veal scaloppini and mushrooms in the skillet. Add wine, cream, salt and pepper. Continue cooking for 4 to 10 minutes. Remove the veal scaloppini and place it on a platter; keep warm. Continue to reduce the sauce over low heat.

When ready to serve, pour the sauce over the veal scaloppini. Serve with vegetables.

Serves 6

Preparation Time: 30 minutes
Cooking Time: 15 to 20 minutes

Sella Di Vitello

(Roast Saddle of Veal)

A savory sauce of mushroom juices, pan juices, chicken broth and wine enhances this tender veal roast.

5-6 lb. (2.3-2.7 kg) veal roast (saddle)

salt & pepper to taste

1 cup *(250 mL)* thickly sliced mushrooms

½ cup *(125 mL)* medium-diced onion

1 cup *(250 mL)* chicken broth, see page 12

1 cup *(250 mL)* white wine

*P*lace the veal roast in a large roasting pan or baking dish and season well with salt and pepper.

Place in a 400°F (200°C) oven and roast for 40 to 50 minutes, until medium or well done.

Add mushrooms and onions to the pan and continue roasting for at least 5 minutes. Add the broth and wine and let reduce by half.

Remove the roast from the pan and slice. Pour the sauce over and serve.

Serves 6

Preparation Time: 10 minutes
Cooking Time: 45 to 90 minutes

Involtini Di Vitello

(Stuffed Veal)

Sweet and rich, marsala adds a smoky depth to the mushroom stuffing and the capicollo adds a spicy tang. The combination is seductive.

12, 2 oz. (55 g) veal scaloppini

12 slices of capicollo for stuffing

Mushroom Marsala Stuffing

½ lb. (250 g) mozzarella cheese, diced

½ lb. (250 g) cooked mushrooms, finely chopped

1 tbsp. (15 mL) chopped parsley

2 egg yolks

¼ cup (60 mL) marsala wine

¼ cup (60 mL) grated Parmesan cheese

¼ cup (60 mL) white wine

3 tbsp. (15 mL) vegetable oil

flour

¼ cup (60 mL) demi-glace, see page 13

2 tbsp. (30 mL) chicken broth, see page 12

salt & pepper to taste

Pound the veal scaloppini until they are 2 to 3 times larger than their original size. Place 1 piece of capicollo on each piece of veal.

In a large bowl, mix the stuffing ingredients together thoroughly.

Place 1 tsp. (5 mL) of the stuffing in the center of each piece of veal and fold lengthwise. Place a skillet over medium heat and add the oil. Flour the veal and brown on both sides. Set the veal aside and keep warm.

Remove the oil from the pan and add the white wine. Add demi-glace, broth, salt and pepper and reduce the sauce.

Place the veal on individual plates. Pour the sauce over the veal.

Serves 4

Preparation Time: 30 minutes
Cooking Time: 15 minutes

Vitello Alla Parmigiana

(Veal Parmigiana)

The traditional Parmigiana coating includes grated Parmesan cheese mixed with the bread crumbs. In this lighter version of the Italian-American classic, melted mozzarella tops a layer of rich tomato sauce.

6, 4 oz. *(115 g)* veal scaloppini

2 eggs

½ cup *(125 mL)* milk

flour

2 cups *(500 mL)* bread crumbs

⅓ cup *(75 mL)* vegetable oil

3 cups *(750 mL)* tomato sauce, see page 20

12 thin slices mozzarella cheese

Pound the veal scaloppini until the pieces are 2 to 3 times larger than the original size.

In a shallow pan, beat together the eggs and milk. Dredge the veal in flour, then dip it in the egg mixture, and then in the bread crumbs.

In a skillet, heat the oil over high heat. Fry the veal until golden brown; remove from pan and place on a baking sheet. Pour tomato sauce over the veal and lay a slice of mozzarella on top of each scaloppini.

Place in a 400°F (200°C) oven and bake until the cheese is melted.

Serves 6

Preparation Time: 20 minutes
Cooking Time: 10 minutes

Nodini Al Pomodoro E Funghi

(Veal Chops with Tomato & Mushrooms)

Italians have used sage for centuries, in cooking and as a healing plant. The smoky flavor of sage goes very well with rich flavors like mushrooms.

6 veal chops

salt & pepper to taste

¼ cup *(60 mL)* olive oil

1 tbsp. *(15 mL)* butter

1 small onion, finely diced

2 cups *(500 mL)* thickly sliced fresh mushrooms

1 garlic clove, minced

2 sage leaves, fresh or dried, minced

½ cup *(125 mL)* white wine

1 cup *(250 mL)* peeled, diced ripe tomatoes

1 cup *(250 mL)* chicken broth

Season the veal chops on both sides with salt and pepper.

In a large skillet, heat the oil and butter, add veal chops and brown quickly on both sides, turning frequently. Sauté for about 5 minutes.

Remove the veal chops from the skillet and add the onions and mushrooms. Cook until onions become soft, then return the veal to the skillet and stir well. Add garlic, sage, wine and tomatoes. Stir and cook over medium heat for 20 minutes. If the sauce is reducing too much, add the chicken broth.

Place the veal chops on a platter and pour the sauce over. Serve with vegetables or pasta.

Serves 6

Preparation Time: 20 minutes
Cooking Time: 30 minutes

Pictured on page 135.

COTOLLETTE ALLA MILANESE

(BREADED VEAL CHOPS)

Very simple to prepare, this recipe features the true flavor of tender sautéed veal with a crisp light coating.

6 boneless veal chops

salt & pepper to taste

½ cup *(125 mL)* flour

1 egg, beaten

½ cup *(125 mL)* bread crumbs

½ cup *(125 mL)* oil

1 tbsp. butter

*P*ound the veal chops firmly with a flat-surfaced mallet until each chop is 2 to 3 times larger in size.

Season with salt and pepper. Coat both sides of each chop with flour and shake off excess. Then dip into beaten egg. Coat well with bread crumbs.

In a large skillet, heat the oil and butter and add the veal chops. Sauté the chops over medium heat until golden brown, 10 to 15 minutes. Serve with vegetables or pasta.

Serves 6

Preparation Time: 15 minutes
Cooking Time: 20 minutes

Osso Buco

Osso Buco means hollow bone. Veal shanks have a hollow filled with marrow, a great delicacy. This method of cooking ensures tender, moist veal with wonderful flavor.

6 veal shanks (2"/5 cm thick)

salt & pepper to taste

flour

⅓ cup (75 mL) vegetable oil

1 carrot, diced

1 onion, diced

1 celery stalk, diced

2 quarts (2 L) tomato sauce, see page 20

2 quarts (2 L) demi-glace, see page 13

Season the veal shanks with salt and pepper and dredge in flour.

In a large, deep skillet, heat the oil on high. Fry the shanks on both sides until brown. Remove from the pan and place in a 9 x 13" (23 x 33 cm) baking pan.

In the same skillet, with a little oil, sauté carrots, onion and celery. Pat the sautéed vegetables on top of the shanks. Add the tomato sauce and demiglace.

Bake at 375°F (190°C) for 1 ½ hours, or until the meat is tender.

Serves 6

Preparation Time: **15 minutes**
Cooking Time: **1 to 2 hours**
Pictured opposite.

Fegato Di Vitella Con Cipolla

(Calf's Liver with Onions)

Liver and onions are classic companions. This simple presentation is raised to new heights by the addition of lemon.

½ cup (125 mL) olive oil

1 medium onion, very thinly sliced

1 lb. (500 g) calf's liver, thinly sliced

salt & pepper to taste

2 lemons, juice of

In a large heavy skillet, heat the olive oil over high heat and add the onions to the pan. As the onions start to brown, add the liver. Continue cooking on high for 2 minutes. Do NOT overcook. Add salt, pepper and lemon juice. Serve.

Serves 2

Preparation Time: **10 minutes**
Cooking Time: **5 minutes**

Saltimbocca Alla Romana

(Veal with Ham)

In this Roman recipe for Saltimbocca, the veal is not rolled around the filling. The flavor of Saltimbocca is so remarkable, the name means "jump into the mouth".

2 lbs. (*1 kg.*) veal, trimmed, membrane removed

12 fresh sage leaves

12 slices capicolla* or prosciutto

3 tbsp. (*125 mL*) vegetable oil

flour

¼ cup (*60 mL*) white wine

½ cup (*125 mL*) demi-glace

½ cup (*125 mL*) chicken broth, see page 12

Cut the veal into 12 slices. Pound each piece of veal, using a flat-surfaced mallet, until each piece is 3 times larger in size.

Season the veal slices with salt and pepper. Place 1 sage leaf and 1 slice of capicolla on each slice and pound them together.

Heat the oil in a skillet. Flour each side of the veal slices and sauté for approximately 2 to 3 minutes. Continue cooking for another 2 minutes and add the wine, demi-glace and broth.

Remove the veal and place on individual plates. Let the sauce reduce until it is the desired thickness. Pour the sauce over the veal.

Serves 6

Preparation Time: **20 minutes**
Cooking Time: **10 minutes**

* Capicolla is a spiced Italian ham-like meat made from the pork neck or shoulder butt. It is usually served thinly sliced for antipasto.

Pictured opposite.

POLPETTONE

(VEAL MEAT LOAF)

Slice through this tempting meatloaf to reveal a centre made of creamy eggs and spicy capicollo. It has beautiful presentation and terrific flavor.

3 garlic cloves, minced

1 lb. *(500 g)* ground veal

1 tbsp. *(15 mL)* finely chopped fresh parsley

6 eggs

3 cups *(750 mL)* grated Parmesan cheese

salt & pepper to taste

1 tbsp. *(15 mL)* vegetable oil

½ cup chopped capicollo

oil for meat loaf pan

2 cups *(500 mL)* dry white wine

*I*n a large bowl, combine the garlic, veal, parsley, 4 eggs, cheese, salt and pepper. Mix until well blended. Set aside.

Beat 2 eggs. In a skillet, heat the oil and add the beaten eggs. Stir constantly until the eggs are set. Remove from the heat and set aside.

With moistened hands, shape the meat mixture into a large square patty about ½" (1.3 cm) thick. Spread the cooked eggs and chopped capicollo over the meat layer, leaving a ¼" (1 cm) edge. Roll, starting from the outer edge, and form into a loaf.

Pour ¼" (1 cm) of oil into a baking pan and place in a 350°F (180°C) oven. Remove the pan when the oil is heated.

Carefully place the meat loaf in the pan and bake for 50 minutes.

Remove the meat loaf from the oven and pour the wine over it; return to the oven for another 10 minutes. Slice and serve hot.

Serves 4 to 6

Preparation Time: **20 minutes**
Cooking Time: **1 hour**

Bistecca Alla Pizzaiola

(Beef in Wine & Tomato Sauce)

Naples is where this tender succulent beef and tomato dish originated.

3 tbsp. *(45 mL)* olive oil

8, 4 oz. *(115 g)* beef tenderloins*

2 garlic cloves, minced

½ cup *(125 mL)* dry white wine

28 oz. *(796 mL)* can tomatoes, chopped with liquid

salt & pepper to taste

Heat the oil in a large skillet over high heat. When the oil is hot, sauté the beef tenderloin for about 2 minutes per side. Remove from the skillet and set aside. Keep warm.

In the same skillet, combine the garlic, wine, tomatoes, salt and pepper. Simmer for 15 minutes over low heat, stirring frequently.

Return the tenderloin to the skillet and continue to simmer for another 10 minutes (or longer if you prefer the tenderloin well done).

When ready to serve, place the tenderloins on individual plates and pour the sauce over.

Serves 4

Preparation Time: 15 minutes
Cooking Time: 30 minutes

* Beef tenderloin is the most tender, choice cut of beef. It is most economical to purchase a whole tenderloin or filet and cut it into individual portions.

If your wallet does not extend to tenderloin, sirloin is an acceptable substitute.

Filetto Di Manzo Al Vino Rosso

(Beef in Red Wine Sauce)

The full-bodied flavor of red wine and the mild onion accent of shallots create a sophisticated, delicious sauce for this tender beef and mushroom dish.

4 tbsp. *(60 mL)* olive oil

12, 4 oz. *(115 g)* beef tenderloins*

1 lb. *(500 g)* thickly sliced fresh mushrooms

4 shallots, finely sliced

salt & pepper to taste

1 ½ cups *(375 mL)* dry red wine

3 tbsp. *(45 mL)* butter

Heat the oil in a large skillet over high heat. When the oil is hot, sauté the beef tenderloins for about 2 minutes per side. Remove the tenderloins and keep warm.

Add the mushrooms and shallots, let cook for about 5 minutes. Season with salt and pepper. Pour the wine into the skillet and let it boil for about 5 minutes.

Add the butter and stir well. Return the beef to the skillet and continue cooking until the sauce has reduced, 5 to 10 minutes (or longer if you prefer the fillet well done).

When ready to serve, place the tenderloins on individual plates and pour the sauce over.

Serves 6

Preparation Time: 15 minutes
Cooking Time: 20 to 30 minutes

* See the tenderloin note on page 159.

Filetto Di Manzo In Agrodolce

(Sweet & Sour Beef)

The sweet pungent flavor of balsamic vinegar is a highlight in this robust beef tenderloin and mushroom dish.

8, 4 oz. *(115 g)* beef tenderloins*

salt & pepper to taste

2 tbsp. *(30 mL)* butter

2 cups *(500 mL)* sliced mushrooms

¼ cup *(60 mL)* balsamic vinegar

3 cups *(750 mL)* demi-glace, see page 13

1 cup *(250 mL)* beef broth

Season the tenderloins with salt and pepper.

Melt the butter in a heavy skillet and add the fillets. Sauté until they are cooked to your preference**. Remove the fillets from the pan and keep warm.

Add the mushrooms and sauté for 1 to 2 minutes. Add the vinegar, demi-glace, and broth.

Place the tenderloins on a platter or individual plates and pour the sauce over.

Serves 4

Preparation Time: **5 minutes**
Cooking Time: **5 to 20 minutes**

* See the tenderloin note on page 159.

** Cooking Times (approximate):

1" (2.5 cm) tenderloin – RARE, 6 to 8 minutes; MEDIUM-RARE, 8 to 10 minutes; MEDIUM, 10 to 12 minutes.

2" (5 cm) tenderloin – RARE, 12 to 14 minutes; MEDIUM-RARE, 14 to 18 minutes; MEDIUM, 18 to 20 minutes.

TRUFFLED FILET

Truffle oil is an excellent way to experience the magnificent flavor of truffles without breaking the bank. This presentation is a visual feast worthy of the inspired combination of flavors.

⅓ lb. *(150 g)* field greens or lettuces of your choice

4 tbsp. *(60 mL)* extra-virgin olive oil

3 tbsp. *(45 mL)* red wine vinegar

salt & freshly ground pepper

Parmesan cheese in a wedge or block

6, 6 oz. *(170 g)* filet* mignon steaks

black or white truffle oil to drizzle

Wash and dry the greens. In a small bowl, whisk together the olive oil, vinegar, salt and pepper. Set aside.

Make shavings of Parmesan cheese with a vegetable peeler. Set aside.

Grill individual steaks to your liking, see page 145.

When the steaks are done, toss the greens with the dressing. Divide the salad among 6 plates and center the steaks on top. Add salt and pepper to taste.

Drizzle each steak with truffle oil. Top each serving with Parmesan cheese slivers and serve immediately.

Serves 6

Preparation Time: 20 minutes
Cooking Time: 5 to 10 minutes

* Filet is the French spelling for a boneless piece of meat or fish, North Americans use fillet. Filet Mignon is a specific cut of beef from the small end of a beef tenderloin, usually 2 to 3" (5 to 7.5 cm) wide and 1 ½ to 2" thick.

Bistecca Alla Zingara

(Beef Gypsy Style)

Peppers, mushrooms and Marsala, this rich lively combination of flavors is bursting with flavor.

2 tbsp. *(30 mL)* olive oil

4, 8 oz. *(250 g)* New York steaks

1 red pepper, sliced

1 green pepper, sliced

1 cup *(250 mL)* sliced mushrooms

½ cup *(125 mL)* Marsala wine

2 cups *(500 mL)* demi-glace, see
   page 13

salt & pepper to taste

1 tsp. *(5 mL)* chopped parsley

Heat the oil in a large, heavy sauté pan. Add the steaks and cook as desired, see page 133. Remove the steaks from the pan and keep warm.

Add the peppers and mushrooms. Sauté for 2 minutes. Deglaze the pan with Marsala wine; add demi-glace, salt and pepper. Bring to a boil and add parsley.

Place the steaks on a platter and pour the sauce over the beef.

Serves 4

Preparation Time: 10 minutes
Cooking Time: 10 to 20 minutes

Steak Al Pepe

(Pepper Steak)

This zesty marinade creates a tender beef dish with marvellous flavor. Peppers, tomatoes and mushrooms add flavor and gorgeous color.

1 lb. *(500 g)* steak, round or sirloin

2 tbsp. *(30 mL)* Worcestershire sauce

1 tbsp. *(15 mL)* lemon juice

1 tbsp. *(15 mL)* Tamari soy sauce

dash freshly ground pepper

1 tbsp. *(15 mL)* whole-wheat flour or cornstarch

1 tbsp. *(15 mL)* olive oil

½ cup *(125 mL)* red wine or water

1 cup *(250 mL)* slivered green pepper

1 small onion, sliced

1 cup *(250 mL)* sliced mushrooms

2 tomatoes, cut in wedges

Cut the meat into thin strips.

Combine the Worcestershire sauce, lemon juice, soy sauce and pepper. Add the meat and flour, stirring to coat the meat. Marinate for 2 to 3 hours. Drain the meat well.

In a large skillet, heat the oil and sauté the meat until browned. Stir in the wine and marinade; cover and simmer for 1 ½ hours.

Add green peppers, onion and mushrooms, simmer gently until peppers are tender and still crunchy, about 4 to 5 minutes. Remove from the heat and stir in tomatoes. Put back on the heat for another 5 minutes.

Serve over rice. If done properly, the meat should be very tender and the vegetables should enhance the entrée.

Serves 6

Preparation Time: **4 hours**
Cooking Time: **2 hours**

VEGETABLES
& RICE

Asparagi Alla Besciamella

(Asparagus in Béchamel Sauce)

Beautiful presentation and fabulous flavors. This asparagus dish is a treat for all of the senses.

3 lbs. *(1.5 kg)* fresh asparagus

¼ cup *(60 mL)* soft butter

¼ lb. *(115 g)* prosciutto thinly sliced

2 cups *(500 mL)* Béchamel sauce, see page 15

½ cup *(125 mL)* grated Parmesan cheese

Wash the asparagus and scrape the stems with a knife.

Arrange the asparagus in a bunch with the tips even. Tie together at the bottom with thread and even off the ends by slicing with a sharp knife.

Stand the asparagus, tips up, in a tall pot. Add enough cold water to cover the stems. Bring to a boil, then reduce heat and simmer for 10 minutes. Do not cover.

Remove the pot from the heat and transfer the asparagus to a chopping board. Untie and cut off the hard white ends.

Place the asparagus in a shallow dish and add the butter, mixing well. Wrap slices of prosciutto around bundles of 3 or 4 spears and place in a buttered baking dish. Cover with Béchamel sauce and sprinkle with grated Parmesan cheese.

Bake at 350°F (180°C) for 15 to 20 minutes, or until golden brown.

Serves 6

Preparation Time: 30 minutes
Cooking Time: 30 minutes

Asparagi In Salsa Maionese

(Asparagus with Mayonnaise)

Fresh asparagus is a true delight. The natural asparagus flavor needs little enhancement, this zesty lemony mayonnaise is perfect.

MAYONNAISE

6 egg yolks

2 cups olive oil

1 lemon, juice of

Tabasco to taste

Worcestershire sauce

salt & pepper to taste

30 cooked asparagus stalks, fresh or frozen

Place the egg yolks in a large mixing bowl and slowly whisk in the oil until completely absorbed.

Whisk in the lemon juice, Tabasco, Worcestershire, salt and pepper.

Divide the asparagus among 6 plates and pour a little of the mayonnaise over the asparagus.

Serves 6

Preparation Time: 15 minutes

* See page 166 for asparagus cooking instructions.

Zucchini Al Pomodoro

(Zucchini with Tomato)

Small (young) zucchini have a light, delicate flavor. In this recipe, tomato sauce, garlic and wine add color and robust flavor.

1 small zucchini

1 tbsp. *(15 mL)* butter

1 garlic clove, crushed

¼ cup *(60 mL)* white wine

½ cup *(125 mL)* tomato sauce, see page 20

salt & pepper to taste

Slice the zucchini into ½" (1.5 cm) slices.

Place the butter in a skillet over medium heat and sauté the zucchini for 2 minutes.

Add the garlic and wine and let cook for another 30 seconds. Add the tomato sauce, salt and pepper. Cook for another 2 minutes and serve.

Serves 2

Preparation Time: 5 minutes
Cooking Time: 5 minutes

Frittata Con Spinaci

(Spinach Omelet)

Colorful and tasty, this frittata is perfect for brunch, lunch or a light dinner.

9 eggs

2 cups *(500 mL)* chopped fresh spinach

2 tbsp. *(30 mL)* finely chopped onion

2 tbsp. *(30 mL)* milk

1 tsp. *(5 mL)* salt

½ tsp. *(2 mL)* dried basil

1 garlic clove, finely minced

8 slices tomato

1 cup *(250 mL)* shredded mozzarella cheese

*I*n a large bowl, beat the eggs until light and fluffy.

Stir in the spinach, onion, milk, salt, basil and garlic.

Pour into a greased 7" x 11" (18 x 28 cm) baking dish. Arrange tomato slices on top; sprinkle with cheese.

Bake, uncovered, at 350°F (180°C) until set, 25 to 30 minutes.

Serves 8

Preparation Time:
Cooking Time: 25 to 30 minutes

Frittata Con Carciofi

(Artichoke Omelette)

The ancient Romans cherished the artichoke. It was considered food for the nobles. Hearty, sharp accompanying flavors bring out the best flavors in the artichokes. This sausage and garlic combination is bursting with flavor.

4 pork sausages, sliced

½ onion, chopped

1 garlic clove, crushed

6 oz. *(170 g)* can of artichokes sliced

salt & pepper to taste

4 eggs, beaten

⅓ cup *(75 mL)* Parmesan cheese

1 tsp. *(5 mL)* chopped parsley

*I*n a large skillet, sauté the sausage, onions and garlic.

Add the artichokes, salt and pepper. Stir in the eggs and pour into a buttered 5 x 7" (13 x 18 cm) baking dish. Sprinkle the cheese and parsley over the eggs.

Bake at 350°F (180°C) for 20 minutes.

Serves 4

Preparation Time: 10 minutes
Cooking Time: 30 minutes

CARCIOFI FRITTI

(FRIED ARTICHOKES)

Serve these crisp flavorful morsels as a side dish or as an appetizer. Delicious.

1 lemon, juice of

6 tender artichokes*

1 egg, beaten

flour

vegetable oil for frying

salt to taste

Put the lemon juice into a bowl of cold water. Wash the artichokes and trim off the outer leaves and the stems. Slice the artichokes vertically into quarters and immediately drop the quarters into the water/lemon mixture.

In a medium saucepan, heat oil until very hot, 365 to 375°F (185 to 190°C).

Dip the artichokes into the beaten egg, then roll in flour to coat. Shake off excess.

Fry the artichokes until crispy and golden brown. Sprinkle with salt and serve.

Serves 4

Preparation Time: **20 minutes**
Cooking Time: **10 minutes**

* Artichokes are members of the thistle family (sometimes called globe artichokes). They may affect the flavors of other foods and wine because they have a chemical called cynarin. Garlic, citrus, olives, capers, vinegars, basil and oregano are some of the flavors that bring out the best in artichokes.

Cavoletti Di Bruxelle, Con Pancetta, Alla Vastese

(Brussels Sprouts with Bacon)

Thie rich salty flavor of bacon gives these tender Brussels sprouts a distinctive flavor.

1 lb. *(500 g)* fresh Brussels sprouts

¼ lb. *(115 g)* bacon, chopped

1 tbsp. *(15 mL)* butter

salt & pepper to taste

Place the washed brussel sprouts in a saucepan with a small amount of boiling salted water. Cook for about 15 minutes, or until tender. Drain.

In a medium saucepan, melt the butter over high heat. Add the bacon and fry for about 10 minutes.

Stir in the Brussels sprouts, salt and pepper. Continue cooking for about 5 minutes before serving.

Serves 4

Preparation Time: 5 minutes
Cooking Time: 15 minutes

Broccoli Romani Al'Aglio

(Fried Broccoli)

Broccoli is one of the most healthful vegetables and one of the most beautiful. Seasoned with garlic and wine, this dish is outstanding.

1 bunch broccoli

3 tbsp. *(45 mL)* olive oil

2 garlic cloves, minced

salt & pepper to taste

½ cup *(125 mL)* dry white wine

Wash the broccoli and cut into florets.

Add broccoli to a large saucepan of boiling, salted water and cook just until the florets are bright green and the stems are soft.

Heat the oil in a medium saucepan. Add garlic and sauté until light brown. Add the broccoli and sprinkle with salt and pepper. Sauté for 2 minutes. Pour the wine over and continue cooking for another 2 minutes.

Serves 4

Preparation Time: 5 minutes
Cooking Time: 10 minutes

Cavolfiore Alla Milanese

(Fried Cauliflower)

Crisp, golden cauliflower florets have crunchy texture and mellow flavor.

1 large cauliflower

flour

2 eggs, beaten

bread crumbs

¼ cup *(60 mL)* oil

3 tbsp. *(45 mL)* butter

salt to taste

Remove the outer leaves from the cauliflower. In a large saucepan, bring water to a boil and add the cauliflower whole. Cook for about 15 minutes. Drain.

Cool the cauliflower and break into florets.

Dip the cauliflower into flour and then into the egg. Coat with the breadcrumbs.

In a large skillet, heat the oil and butter until very hot. Add the cauliflower; reduce the heat and fry for 10 minutes, or until golden brown.

Serves 6

Preparation Time: **20 minutes**
Cooking Time: **30 minutes**

Pepperoni Alla Romana

(Peppers Stuffed with Pasta)

Peppers are beautiful natural containers that can be stuffed with many different fillings. Use your imagination and also use red or yellow peppers if you prefer. These peppers are superb.

4 large sweet green peppers

4 quarts *(4 L)* water

2 tbsp. *(30 mL)* salt

2 cups *(500 mL)* orchichetti*

3 cups *(750 mL)* meat sauce, see page 19

¼ cup *(60 mL)* Parmesan cheese

⅓ cup *(75 mL)* chopped chives or green onions

½ tsp. *(2 mL)* dried oregano

dash hot pepper flakes (optional)

salt & pepper to taste

¾ cup *(175 mL)* grated mozzarella cheese

Remove and save the tops of the peppers. Core and seed peppers. Blanch peppers and tops in boiling water for 5 minutes. This makes them tender.

In a large pot, bring the water and salt to a boil. Add the pasta and cook, uncovered, stirring occasionally until pasta is al dente, about 6 to 8 minutes. Drain well.

Combine the hot, cooked pasta with 1 ½ cups (375 mL) of the spaghetti sauce, Parmesan cheese, chives, oregano, pepper flakes, salt and pepper.

Stuff each pepper with the pasta mixture. Top each pepper with grated mozzarella cheese and replace the pepper lids.

Stand the peppers in a baking dish and pour the remaining sauce around them. Cover the dish with foil and bake at 375°F (190°C) for 30 minutes, or until tender but not limp. Serve immediately.

Serves 4

Preparation Time: 30 minutes
Cooking Time: 45 minutes

* Orchichetti are very small disk-shaped pasta, "little ears". If you can not find them, substitute baby pasta shells.

Patate Alla Paesana

(Fried Potatoes with Onion)

Hearty. aromatic and delicious, these are the ultimate in fried potatoes.

2 lbs. *(1 kg)* potatoes

¼ cup *(60 mL)* olive oil

2 tbsp. *(30 mL)* butter

3 onions, thickly sliced

salt & pepper to taste

Peel the potatoes and slice thinly.

In a large skillet, heat the olive oil and butter. Add the onions and sauté until soft.

Add the potatoes and season with salt and pepper. Fry for abut 30 minutes over medium heat, stirring frequently.

Serves 6

Preparation Time: 10 minutes
Cooking Time: 40 to 50 minutes

Patate Al Lesso

(Boiled Potatoes)

This is very basic, but it's hard to beat the flavor of simple boiled potatoes.

2 lbs. *(1 kg)* potatoes

salt to taste

2 tbsp. *(30 mL)* finely chopped fresh parsley

Peel the potatoes and cut in medium-sized pieces.

In a large pot, bring salted water to a boil. Add the potatoes and cook over low heat for about 35 minutes. Drain.

Place the potatoes in a serving bowl and sprinkle with parsley. Mix well.

Serves 6

Preparation Time: 5 minutes
Cooking Time: 35 to 50 minutes

L'Aglio Arosto

(Roasted Garlic Mashed Potatoes)

Creamy and savory, garlicy mashed potatoes are unforgettable.

2 lbs. *(1 kg)* baking potatoes, peeled and cut into large chunks

1 tbsp. *(15 mL)* unsalted butter

½ cup *(125 mL)* heavy cream

½ cup *(125 mL)* Consorzio roasted garlic olive oil

salt & pepper to taste

2 tbsp. *(30 mL)* chopped chives

Cook the potatoes in a large pot of boiling, salted water until fork tender. Drain and let them dry on a baking pan for 5 minutes.

In a large bowl, using an electric mixer, begin mashing the potatoes with the butter. Heat the cream just to boiling; add to the potatoes and continue to beat.

Beat in the roasted garlic olive oil. Season with salt and pepper to taste. Beat in the chives.

If too thick, thin with warm milk. Reheat if necessary (this is most easily done in a microwave oven).

Serves 4

Preparation Time: 10 minutes
Cooking Time: 15 minutes

PATATE AL FORNO CON ROSMARINO

(ROASTED POTATOES WITH ROSEMARY)

The caramelized flavor of roasted potatoes is wonderful with the aromatic addition of rosemary.

2 lbs. *(1 kg)* potatoes, thinly sliced

½ cup *(125 mL)* olive oil

4 tbsp. *(60 mL)* butter

salt to taste

2 tsp. *(10 mL)* dried rosemary

Peel the potatoes and slice thinly.

In a large, ovenproof skillet, heat the oil and butter until very hot.

Add the potatoes and sprinkle with salt and rosemary. Sauté for about 5 minutes, stirring constantly.

Place the skillet in the oven and roast at 350°F (180°C) for 30 minutes, stirring occasionally.

Serves 6

Preparation Time: 10 minutes
Cooking Time: 35 to 50 minutes

Risotto Con Scampi

(Rice with Scampi)

This luxurious risotto is rich and creamy. Sophisticated and yet easy to make, it is exceptional.

2 lbs. *(500 g)* scampi, medium size, in shells

2 quarts *(2 L)* water

___salt

Rice

1 tbsp. *(15 mL)* butter

¼ cup *(60 mL)* olive oil

½ medium onion, diced

5 cups *(1.25 L)* Arborio rice (Italian short-grain rice)

Creamy Tomato Sauce with Scampi & Brandy

2 tbsp. *(30 mL)* butter

5 medium shallots, diced

1 garlic clove, minced

salt & pepper to taste

1 tbsp. *(15 mL)* parsley

½ cup *(125 mL)* brandy

2 cups *(500 mL)* whipping cream

5 cups *(1.25 L)* tomato sauce, see page 20

Split the scampi in half and remove the shells. Set the scampi aside. In a large saucepan, bring the water to a boil, add the salt and scampi shells; boil for 20 minutes.

Rice: Meanwhile, in a large skillet, heat the butter and oil and sauté the onion over medium heat for about 5 minutes. Add the rice and stir well.

Strain the scampi broth and discard the shells. Add the broth to the rice and stir well with a wooden spoon. Cover and cook for 20 minutes.

Sauce: In a skillet, melt the butter and sauté the shallots and garlic over medium heat for 5 minutes. Add the scampi and stir well. Add the salt, pepper, and parsley. Cook for another 5 minutes.

Remove the skillet from the heat and pour the brandy over the scampi. Remove the scampi and return the skillet to the heat.

Add the whipping cream, tomato sauce and stir well. Cook for 15 minutes, stirring occasionally.

Add the rice and scampi to the sauce and stir well.

Serves 6 to 8

Preparation Time: 20 minutes
Cooking Time: 40 minutes

Pictured on page 155.

RISOTTO PORTOFINO

(RICE WITH SHRIMP SAUCE)

This risotto is bursting with flavor and color, tomato sauce, shrimp, mushrooms and green peas.

2 quarts *(2 L)* water

1 ½ - 2 tsp. *(7 - 10 mL)* salt

3 cups *(750 mL)* Arborio rice
  (Italian short-grain rice)

3 tbsp. *(15 mL)* olive oil

1 lb. *(500 g)* shrimp

1 ½ cups *(375 mL)* sliced
  mushrooms

2 garlic cloves, crushed

¼ cup *(60 mL)* white wine

2 tbsp. *(30 mL)* chopped parsley

1 cup *(250 mL)* green peas

6 cups *(1.5 L)* tomato sauce, see
  page 20

salt & pepper to taste

1 cup *(250 mL)* Parmesan cheese

*I*n a large saucepan, bring the water to a boil. Add the salt and rice and cover. Cook for 20 minutes.

Meanwhile, in a large skillet, heat the oil and sauté the shrimp, mushrooms, and garlic together for approximately 1 minute. Add the wine, parsley, green peas, tomato sauce, salt and pepper. Simmer for an additional 2 minutes. Remove half of the mushroom sauce from the pan and set aside.

Drain the rice and add it to the sauce in the pan. Stir in the cheese.

Place the rice on individual plates and add the shrimp. Pour the remaining sauce over.

Serves 4

Preparation Time: 20 minutes
Cooking Time: 30 minutes

Risotto Pescatora

(Fisherman's Rice)

This bountiful array of seafood creates an incredibly elegant rice dish. Complex flavors seductive aroma – enjoy!

1 lb. *(500 g)* baby clams

12 large shrimp, shelled, deveined

12 large squid, cleaned

½ cup *(125 mL)* olive oil

1 tbsp. *(15 mL)* butter

1 medium onion, diced

1 garlic clove, minced

½ cup *(125 mL)* dry white wine

½ lb. *(250 g)* fresh mushrooms, thinly sliced

salt & pepper to taste

4 cups *(1 L)* Arborio rice, (Italian short-grain rice)

2 quarts *(2 L)* chicken broth, see page 12

Wash and scrub the clams. Slice the shrimp into bite-sized pieces. Cut the squid crosswise into ¾" (2 cm) thick pieces.

In a large saucepan, heat the oil and butter; sauté the onion and garlic for 5 minutes, then add the seafood. Stir well. Cook for another 5 minutes.

Add the wine and simmer for 10 minutes. Add a little water and stir occasionally.

Add mushrooms, salt and pepper. Stir well. Remove the clams.

Add the rice and chicken broth. Continue cooking for 20 minutes, stirring occasionally. When ready to serve garnish the rice with the clams.

Serves 6 to 8

Preparation Time: 20 minutes
Cooking Time: 40 minutes

Risotto Con Funghi

(Rice with Mushrooms)

Deliciously creamy rice flavored with onions and mushrooms.

⅓ cup *(75 mL)* butter

1 onion, diced

2 cups *(500 mL)* finely sliced fresh mushrooms

8-10 cups *(2 - 2.5 L)* chicken broth, see page 12

4 cups *(1 L)* Arborio rice (Italian short-grain rice)

¼ cup *(60 mL)* grated Parmesan cheese

*I*n a large saucepan, melt the butter over medium heat and sauté the onion. When the onion becomes soft, stir in the mushrooms. Add the chicken broth and bring to a boil. Stir in the rice. Do NOT cover.

Reduce the heat and cook for 30 minutes, or until the rice is tender. Stir frequently.

Remove the rice from the heat. Stir in the remaining butter and the grated Parmesan cheese.

Serves 6

Preparation Time: **10 minutes**
Cooking Time: **40 minutes**

Risotto Zafferano

(Rice with Saffron)

Risotto with saffron is a famous Milanese specialty. The distinctive color, flavor and fragrance of saffron adds a luxurious note to this succulent dish.

1 ½ cups (375 mL) chicken broth,
  see page 12

½ cup (125 mL) Arborio rice
  (Italian short-grain rice)

salt & pepper to taste

pinch of saffron

¼ cup (60 mL) Parmesan cheese

*I*n a small saucepan, bring the chicken broth to a boil and add the rice. Cook for approximately 20 minutes, stirring continuously.

Add the salt, pepper and saffron. Then stir in the Parmesan cheese. Cook until the rice becomes sticky, about 5 minutes, and serve.

Serves 2

Preparation Time: 5 minutes
Cooking Time: 25 minutes

* Saffron is native to Asia Minor. Used in ancient Persia, 3,500 years ago, it was exported to Kashmir and then to Europe. Today most saffron is exported from Iran, Spain and India. Saffron is the red stigma of the autumn crocus flower, and as there are only 3 stigmas per flower, it takes approximately 2,000 plants to make a ½ ounce (15 g) of saffron. This is the world's most expensive spice but it provides a wonderful mellow flavor and only a small amount is needed per recipe. Saffron has been used as a flavoring for thousands of years. Distinctive dishes in many cultures depend upon the use of saffron, Risotto Milanese, Bouillabaisse and Paella are three of the most famous.

CROCANTE

(RICE CROQUETTES)

Crisp and golden on the outside, these croquettes are soft and tender inside.

4 cups *(1 L)* Arborio rice (Italian short-grain rice)

2 quarts *(2 L)* water

3 eggs

2 cups *(500 mL)* Parmesan cheese

3 tbsp. *(45 mL)* chopped parsley

2 cups *(500 mL)* bread crumbs

salt & pepper to taste

2 cups *(500 mL)* olive oil

*I*n a large saucepan, bring the rice and water to a boil. Cook the rice for 20 minutes. Drain the rice and refrigerate for approximately 3 hours.

Mix the rice with the eggs, Parmesan cheese, parsley, bread crumbs, salt and pepper. Make sure the mixture is fairly stiff. Add more bread crumbs if necessary.

Form the rice mixture into 1 ½" (4 cm) balls.

Heat the oil to 365 to 375°F (185 to 190°C) and fry the croquettes, a few at a time, until golden brown, about 10 minutes per batch.

Serves 8

Preparation Time: 4 hours
Cooking Time: 30 minutes

BREADS

POLENTA

(CORNMEAL)

In northern Italy, Polenta is a staple. It is served hot with butter as a side dish or for breakfast. It can also be chilled, cut into squares and grilled or fried.

4 *(1 L)* cups water

2 tbsp. *(30 mL)* salt

½ cup *(125 mL)* olive oil

3 cups *(750 mL)* fine cornmeal

¼ cup *(60 mL)* Parmesan cheese

Bring the water to a boil and add the salt and oil.

Slowly whisk in the cornmeal and cook over low heat for 1 hour.

Serve with tomato sauce and cod fish, or zucchini, or sausage and sprinkle with additional cheese.

Serves 6

Preparation Time: 20 minutes
Cooking Time: 1 hour

RICE FLOUR QUICK BREAD

No eggs, no milk, this wheat-flour-free bread is ideal for people with wheat and egg allergies.

2 tbsp. + 2 tsp. *(40 mL)*
                 egg substitute

2 cups *(500 mL)* milk

2 tsp. *(10 mL)* baking powder

2 tsp. *(10 mL)* baking soda

¼ cup *(60 mL)* sugar

4 cups *(1 L)* pure rice flour

In a large bowl, beat together all of the ingredients, except the flour. Fold in the rice flour.

Pour the batter into a greased 4 x 8" (10 x 20 cm) loaf pan and bake at 350°F (180°C) for 45 minutes. Cool on a wire rack.

Makes 1 loaf

Preparation Time: 5 minutes
Cooking Time: 45 minutes

Corn Bread

Corn Bread is delicious served warm with hearty meat dishes or for breakfast. The crust is slightly crunchy and the texture has a slightly gritty quality. Addictive!

2 cups *(500 mL)* cornmeal

1 cup *(250 mL)* corn flour

1 cup *(250 mL)* rice flour

½ tsp. *(2 mL)* salt

1 tsp. *(5 mL)* baking soda

2 tsp. *(10 mL)* baking powder

3 eggs

⅓ cup *(75 mL)* cooking oil

2 ¼ *(550 mL)* cups buttermilk

*I*n a large bowl, combine the cornmeal, flours, salt, baking soda and baking powder.

In a separate bowl, beat the eggs until frothy, then whisk in the oil and buttermilk.

Add the wet ingredients to the dry ingredients, mixing just until blended.

Pour the batter into a waxed-paper-lined 9" (23 cm) square baking pan and bake at 350°F (180°C) for 45 minutes.

Test for doneness before taking out of the oven. Cut in squares to serve. If not serving immediately, warm for 45 seconds in a microwave before serving.

Serves 9

Preparation Time: 10 minutes
Cooking Time: 45 minutes

POTATO RICE BREAD

This bread uses potato flour and brown rice flour – no wheat flour – so it is great for anyone with wheat allergies.

⅓ cup *(75 mL)* pure potato flour

3 cups *(750 mL)* pure brown rice flour

¼ cup *(60 mL)* sugar

1 ½ tsp. *(7 mL)* salt

⅔ cup *(150 mL)* dry milk

1 tbsp. *(15 mL)* instant dry yeast

2 large eggs

¼ cup *(60 mL)* shortening, melted

1 ¾ cups *(425 mL)* warm water

*I*n a large bowl, combine the dry ingredients, including the yeast. Set aside.

Whip the eggs until frothy. Add the shortening and warm water.

Thoroughly mix the dry ingredients into the liquid mixture.

Divide the dough in 2 and place into 2, 4 x 8" (10 x 20 cm) greased loaf pans. Let rise in a warm oven, 200°F (93°C), for 1 hour, or until the bread reaches the top of the pan.

Bake at 400°F (200°C) for 45 minutes.

Makes 2 loaves

Preparation Time: **10 minutes**
Rising Time: **1 hour**
Cooking Time: **45 minutes**

White Bread Rolls

Italian bread is legendary. These rolls take time but try them and see for yourself.

3 lbs. *(1.4 kg)* flour (9 cups *(2.25 L)*

2 cups *(500 mL)* water

½ cup *(125 mL)* sugar

3 tbsp. *(45 mL)* salt

2 eggs, beaten

3 tbsp. *(45 mL)* instant dry yeast

½ cup *(125 mL)* olive oil

*I*n a large bowl, combine all ingredients. Knead for 1 hour or more, until the dough is shiny.

Let rise for 4 hours.

Shape the dough into small rolls and place on an ungreased baking sheet; let rise again for 1 hour.

Bake at 350°F (180°C) for 1 hour (you may reduce heat to 325°F (160°C) after the first half hour).

Makes approximately 12 rolls

Preparation Time: 1hour and 15 minutes
Rising Time: 4 hours
Cooking Time: 1 hour

Bran Brown Bread

This delicious, moist bread may be used at any meal as well as for sandwiches. Housewives used to cool their bread by leaning it against a shelf, and if a crusty outside was desired they allowed the wind to blow over it as it cooled.

2 tsp. *(10 mL)* sugar

½ cup *(125 mL)* lukewarm water

2 tbsp. *(30 mL)* dry granular yeast

¼ cup *(60 mL)* shortening

⅓ cup *(75 mL)* packed brown sugar

2 tbsp. *(30 mL)* molasses

2 tsp. *(10 mL)* salt

1 cup *(250 mL)* milk

1 cup *(250 mL)* water

2 cups *(500 mL)* natural cooking bran

2 cups *(500 mL)* all-purpose flour

3 cups *(750 mL)* whole-wheat flour

Dissolve the sugar in the lukewarm water and sprinkle with the yeast. Set aside to proof for 10 minutes.

In the meantime, with an electric mixer, cream together the shortening, brown sugar, molasses and salt. Add the milk, water and bran. Beat until well blended.

Stir in the yeast when dissolved. Add the all-purpose flour and gradually work in the whole-wheat flour.

Turn out onto a floured board and knead for 10 to 12 minutes using as much more flour as necessary to prevent the dough from sticking to the board.

Cover and set in a warm place to rise until doubled in bulk, approximately 1½ hours.

Punch down the dough and form into 1 large loaf or 2 small loaves. Place in greased 2, 4 x 8" (10 x 20 cm) loaf pans or into 1, 5 x 9" (13 x 23 cm) loaf pan.

Let rise in a warm place until doubled, about ½ hour.

For the large loaf bake at 375°F (190°C) for 40 to 45 minutes, about 30 to 35 minutes for smaller loaves. Cool on racks.

Makes 1 large or 2 small loaves

DESSERTS

GRANITA

(FLAVORED ICES)

Italian ices or granita are superb. The intense flavors and granular texture are delicious and refreshing.

LEMON ICE

2 cups (*500 mL*) water

1 cup (*250 mL*) sugar

1 cup (*250 mL*) lemon juice

ORANGE ICE

2 cups (*500 mL*) water

¾ cup (*175 mL*) sugar

1 cup (*250 mL*) orange juice

1 lemon, juice of

COFFEE ICE

1 cup (*250 mL*) water

½ cup (*125 mL*) sugar

2 cups (*500 mL*) strong espresso coffee

STRAWBERRY ICE

1 cup (*250 mL*) water

½ cup (*125 mL*) sugar

2 cups (*500 mL*) fresh ripe strawberries, puréed through a sieve

2 tbsp. (*30 mL*) lemon juice

*F*or any of these Ice recipes: In a 2-quart (2 L) saucepan, bring the water and sugar to a boil over moderate heat, stirring only until the sugar dissolves. Timing from the moment the sugar and water begin to boil, let the mixture cook for exactly 5 minutes. Immediately remove the pan from the heat and let the syrup cool to room temperature.

Depending on which of the flavored ices you want to make, stir in the lemon juice, or the orange and lemon juices, or the espresso coffee, or the puréed strawberries and lemon juice. Pour the mixture into an ice-cube tray from which the divider has been removed.

Freeze the granita for 3 to 4 hours, stirring it every 30 minutes and scraping into it the ice particles that form around the edges of the tray. The finished granita should have a fine, snowy texture. For a coarser texture that is actually more to the Italian taste, leave the ice cube divider in the tray and freeze the granita solid. Then remove the cubes and crush them in an ice crusher.

Note: if you use unsweetened frozen strawberries rather than fresh ones, make the syrup with only ¼ cup of sugar.

Makes about 1 ½ pints (750 mL) of each flavor

Preparation Time: 15 minutes
Cooking Time: 5 minutes
Freezing Time: 3 to 4 hours

Gelato Alla Vaniglia

(Vanilla Ice Cream)

Italian ice cream has been called the best in the world. It is a marvellous experience to stand in front of the display case of a gelateria in Italy and see the rainbow array of gelati and granita. Now you can create your own.

2 cups (500 mL) light cream

2" (5 cm) piece of vanilla bean
OR 1 tsp. (5 mL) vanilla extract

8 egg yolks

½ cup (125 mL) sugar

1 cup (250 mL) whipping cream
(32% m.f.)

*I*n a 2-quart (2 L) enameled or stainless-steel saucepan, bring the light cream and the vanilla bean almost to a boil over low heat. (If you are using vanilla extract, do not add it now.)

Meanwhile, combine the egg yolks and sugar in a bowl. Beat them with a whisk, rotary or electric beater for 3 to 5 minutes, or until they are pale yellow and thick enough to fall from the whisk or beater in a lazy ribbon. Then discard the vanilla bean and pour the hot cream slowly into the beaten egg yolks, beating gently and constantly. Pour the egg mixture back into the saucepan and cook over moderately low heat, stirring constantly with a wooden spoon, until it thickens to a custard that lightly coats the spoon. Do not allow the custard to boil or it will curdle. Stir in the whipping cream and, if you are using the vanilla extract instead of the vanilla bean, add the extract now. Strain the custard through a fine sieve into a mixing bowl and allow it to cool to room temperature.

Pack a 2-quart (2 L) ice-cream freezer with layers of finely crushed or cracked ice and coarse rock salt in the proportions recommended by the freezer manufacturer. Add cold water if the manufacturer advises it. Pour or ladle the cooled gelato into the ice-cream can and cover it.

If you have a hand ice-cream maker let it stand for 3 to 4 minutes before turning the handle. It may take 15 minutes or more for the ice-cream to freeze, but do not stop turning at any time, or the gelato may be lumpy. When the handle can barely be moved, the ice-cream should be firm. If you have an electric ice-cream maker, turn it on and let it churn for about 15 minutes, or until the motor slows or actually stops.

To harden the gelato, scrape the ice cream from the sides down into the bottom of the can and cover it securely. Drain off any water that is in the bucket and repack it with ice and salt. Let it stand for 2 to 3 hours.

Makes about 1 ½ pints (750 mL)

Gelato Al Pistacchio

(Pistachio Ice Cream)

Pistachios are cultivated in Italy and they are highly valued for their wonderful delicate flavor. They are used in many marvellous desserts and savory dishes.

2 cups *(500 mL)* light cream

8 egg yolks

6 tbsp. *(90 mL)* sugar

2 ½ tbsp. *(37 mL)* ground or crushed, shelled pistachio nuts

1 cup *(250 mL)* whipping cream (32% m.f.)

7 drops green food colouring

5 ½ tbsp. *(82 mL)* chopped, shelled pistachio nuts

¼ cup *(60 mL)* ground blanched almonds

*I*n a 2-quart (2 L) enameled or stainless steel saucepan, heat the light cream.

Beat the egg yolks and sugar together. Add the ground pistachio nuts and make the custard as in the Gelato recipe on page 177.

Then stir in the whipping cream and food coloring. Strain the custard through a fine sieve into a mixing bowl.

Add the chopped pistachio nuts and ground almonds to the custard. Cool.

Freeze as directed on page 195.

Makes about 1 ½ pints (750 mL)

* Buy only pistachio nuts with partially opened shells. When the shells are closed the nuts are not ripe. Pistachios can be addictive, but they are rich in calcium, thiamine, phosphorus, iron and Vitamin A – so indulge.

Gelato Di Caffé

(COFFEE ICE CREAM)

Once you've made this superb gelato. you can adapt it to your coffee preference, a bit more espresso or a bit less or enjoy it as is – fabulous.

2 cups *(500 mL)* light cream

2" *(5 cm)* strip of fresh lemon peel

8 egg yolks

6 tbsp. *(90 mL)* sugar

2 tbsp. *(30 mL)* espresso coffee

2 cups *(500 mL)* whipping cream
   (32% m.f.)

*I*n a 2-quart (2 L) enameled or stainless steel saucepan, heat the light cream with the lemon peel.

Beat the egg yolks and sugar together. Discard the peel and make the custard as in the Gelato recipe, on page 195.

Add the espresso coffee (instant or freshly brewed) and whipping cream; strain the custard through a fine sieve into a mixing bowl and cool.

Freeze as directed on page 195.

Makes about 1 ½ pints (750 mL)

Gelato Al Cioccolato

(CHOCOLATE ICE CREAM)

Theobroma cacao – food of the gods – chocolate is credited with almost magical powers. Always use the best quality chocolate for the best flavor.

2 cups *(500 mL)* milk

4 egg yolks

10 tbsp. *(150 mL)* sugar

2 cups *(500 mL)* whipping cream
   (32% m.f.)

4 oz. *(115 g)* semisweet chocolate,
   melted

½ tsp. *(2 mL)* vanilla extract

*I*n a 2-quart (2 L) enameled or stainless steel saucepan, heat the milk.

Beat the egg yolks and sugar together. Make the custard as in the Gelati recipe on page 193.

Then stir in the whipping cream, melted chocolate and vanilla extract. Strain the custard through a fine sieve into a mixing bowl and cool.

Freeze as directed on page 195.

Makes about 1 1/2 pints (750 mL)

Fragole Semifreddo

(Strawberry Parfait)

Beautiful color and fresh lovely flavor, this dessert is perfect for a summer party.

1 cup (*250 mL*) chopped strawberries

2 tsp. (*10 mL*) water

2 tsp. (*10 mL*) kirsch

2 tbsp. (*30 mL*) sugar

1 cup (*250 mL*) whipping cream

4 egg yolks

In a small enameled or stainless steel saucepan, cook the strawberries with the water, kirsch and 1 tbsp. (15 mL) of sugar for 5 minutes, then cool in the refrigerator.

Whip the cream on high speed until it forms stiff peaks; beat in 1 tbsp. (15 mL) of sugar, then refrigerate.

Whip the egg yolks on high speed until light and lemon coloured. Fold in the whipped cream, strawberries and liquid.

Spoon the strawberry mixture into parfait glasses and freeze for 4 hours. Serve frozen.

Serves 2

Preparation Time: 40 minutes
Cooking Time: 5 minutes

Fragole Al Pepe Verde

(Strawberries with Green Peppercorns)

This combination of flavors is surprising and marvellous. The richness of the Marsala and the sweetness of the strawberries are heightened by the bite of the peppercorns.

1 lb. (*500 g*) strawberries

2 tbsp. (*30 mL*) butter

1 cup (*250 mL*) sugar

1 tsp. (*5 mL*) green peppercorns

½ cup (*125 mL*) Marsala wine

1 lemon, juice of

ice cream for 4

Clean and halve the strawberries.

In a saucepan, melt the butter and add the sugar. Add the strawberries and the peppercorns to the saucepan. Cook for about 1 minute; add the lemon juice and Marsala. Continue cooking the berries for approximately 3 more minutes.

Serve over ice cream.

Serves 4

Preparation Time: 5 minutes
Cooking Time: 5 minutes

Aranci Positano

(Orange Cocktail)

These caramelized oranges sparkle with fresh flavor and gorgeous colour.

1 tbsp. *(15 mL)* butter

¼ cup *(60 mL)* sugar

¼ cup *(60 mL)* thinly sliced orange peel

1 cup *(250 mL)* freshly squeezed orange juice

2 tsp. *(10 mL)* baking soda

4 oz. *(113 mL)* orange liqueur

4 medium oranges, peeled and halved crosswise

In a medium skillet, melt the butter. Add the sugar and orange peel and cook until the sugar browns, about 5 minutes.

Add the orange juice, baking soda and liqueur, mixing well. Cook over medium heat until the sauce thickens and becomes smooth, about 6 minutes.

Add the orange halves and continue cooking for about 3 minutes.

Chill the orange mixture until ready to serve. When ready to serve, place the orange halves in sherbert glasses and pour the sauce over.

Serves 4

Preparation Time: 15 minutes
Cooking Time: 15 minutes

MACEDONIA DI FRUTTA FRESCA

(FRESH FRUIT SALAD)

Light, refreshing and great visual appeal, this dessert is ideal for brunch or a summer evening.

1 grapefruit

1 banana

2 ripe pears

1 apple

1 orange

½ cantaloupe

10 seedless white or red grapes

½ lemon, juice of

3 tbsp. *(45 mL)* sugar

2 oz. *(60 mL)* maraschino liqueur

Wash the fruit, peel and core. Cut into bite-sized pieces and put into a large bowl.

Squeeze the lemon juice over the fruit, then add the sugar and liqueur. Stir well.

Cover and refrigerate for 2 hours, stirring several times.

Serves 4

Preparation Time: 20 minutes

Banana Fritters

A luscious dessert, enjoy the contrast between the hot crunchy, crisp coating and the creamy sweetness of the banana.

1 cup (*250 mL*) flour

1 tsp. (*5 mL*) baking powder

½ tsp. (*2 mL*) salt

½ - ¾ cup (*125 - 175 mL*) milk

1 egg, well beaten

1 quart (*1 L*) vegetable oil for deep-frying

1 or 2 ripe bananas

½ cup (*125 mL*) sugar

1 tbsp. (*15 mL*) rum

*I*n a medium bowl, sift together the flour, baking powder and salt. Add the milk and egg. Beat well.

In a deep saucepan, heat 1 quart (1 L) of oil to 365 to 375°F (185 to 190°C).

Peel the bananas and cut in half lengthwise, then across, making 4 pieces. Carefully drop the bananas into the batter and lift out with a fork (do not pierce) or tongs.

Carefully place the bananas in the hot oil. Fry until nicely browned; drain well on paper towels.

Sprinkle liberally with sugar and rum. Serve hot.

Serves 2 to 4

Preparation Time: 5 minutes
Cooking Time: 5 minutes

Pere Al'Amaretto

(Amaretto Pears)

This elegant dessert is light and has a wonderful flavor and fragrance.

Amaretto Sauce

2 cups (*500 mL*) sugar

1 cup (*250 mL*) warm water

2 cups (*500 mL*) cold water

1 cup (*250 mL*) amaretto liqueur

Poached Pears

2 bay leaves

1 clove

½ lemon

4 cups (*1 L*) water

6 pears, peeled, halved & cored

½ cup (*125 mL*) sugar

Sauce: Combine the sugar and warm water in a saucepan and bring to a boil over high heat. Stir constantly, until the mixture turns a caramel color. Remove from the heat.

Slowly stir in the cold water and amaretto liqueur. Return the pan to the burner; lower the heat and simmer until the sauce has reduced and thickened, about 10 minutes. Remove from the heat and cool. Refrigerate until ready to serve.

Pears: In a saucepan, combine the bay leaves, clove and lemon with the water. Bring to a boil. Add the pears and sugar. Stir and simmer for 30 minutes.

Let the pears cool in the water. When cooled, drain the pears and place in sherbet glasses. Pour the sauce over.

Serves 6

Preparation Time: 15 minutes
Cooking Time: 30 minutes

Pictured on page 211.

CILIEGE AL VINO ROSSO

(BAKED CHERRIES WITH RED WINE)

Brandy and red wine give this cherry dessert a remarkable rich flavor.

1 lb. *(500 g)* ripe cherries

1 tbsp. *(15 mL)* sugar

½ tbsp. *(7 mL)* icing sugar

1 tbsp. *(15 mL)* brandy

1 ½ *(375 mL)* cups red wine

Place the cherries in a shallow baking dish with the sugars, brandy and wine. Bake at 350°F (180°C) for 45 minutes.

Pour the cherry liquid from the baking pan into a saucepan and cook until reduced by half. Pour the sauce over the cherries and let cool for approximately 1 hour before serving.

Serves 4

Preparation Time: 5 minutes
Cooking Time: 1 ½ hours

ZABAGLIONE

(HOT WHIPPED CUSTARD)

Light and frothy, this justly famous Italian dessert is exquisite.

3 egg yolks

½ cup *(125 mL)* sweet Marsala wine

½ cup *(125 mL)* dry white wine

3 tbsp. *(45 mL)* sugar

In a medium saucepan, bring about 1 quart (1 L) of water to a boil over medium heat.

In a stainless steel bowl, combine the egg yolks, Marsala, white wine and sugar. Place the bowl in the saucepan. Tip the bowl slightly toward you and beat the egg mixture with a wire whisk in a backwards and forwards motion. Whisk constantly, until the egg yolks become slightly thickened and light in color.

Pour the Zabaglione into champagne glasses and serve warm.

Serves 6

Preparation Time: 5 minutes
Cooking Time: 5 minutes

Soufflé au Grand Marnier

(Orange Liqueur Soufflé)

Elegant, light and delicious this impressive dessert is truly spectacular.

2 tbsp. *(30 mL)* soft butter

3 tbsp. *(45 mL)* sugar

5 egg yolks

⅓ cup *(75 mL)* sugar

¼ cup *(60 mL)* Grand Marnier

1 tbsp. *(15 mL)* freshly grated
   orange peel

7 egg whites

¼ tsp. *(1 mL)* cream of tartar

confectioner's (powdered) sugar

Grease the bottom and sides of a 1 ½-quart (1.5 L) soufflé dish with 2 tbsp. (30 mL) of soft butter. Sprinkle in 3 tbsp. (45 mL) of sugar, tipping and shaking the dish to spread the sugar evenly. Then turn the dish over and knock out the excess sugar. Set aside.

In the top of a double boiler, beat the egg yolks with a whisk, rotary or electric beater until they are well blended. Slowly add the sugar and continue beating until the yolks become very thick and pale yellow. Set the pan over barely simmering (not boiling) water and heat the egg yolks, stirring gently and constantly with a wooden spoon or rubber spatula, until the mixture thickens and becomes almost too hot to touch. Stir in the Grand Marnier and grated orange peel and transfer to a large bowl. Set the bowl into a pan filled with crushed ice or ice cubes and cold water, and stir the mixture until it is quite cold. Remove it from the ice.

In a large mixing bowl, preferably of unlined copper, beat the egg whites and the cream of tartar with a clean whisk or rotary beater until they form stiff, unwavering peaks. Using a rubber spatula, stir a large spoonful of beaten egg white into the yolk mixture to lighten it. Gently fold the remaining egg whites into the yolk mixture. Spoon the soufflé batter into the buttered, sugared dish, filling it to within 2" (5 cm) of the top. Smooth the top of the soufflé with the spatula. For a decorative effect, make a cap on the soufflé by cutting a trench about 1" deep and 1" (2.5 cm) from the edge all around the top.

Bake at 425°F (220°C) on the middle shelf of the oven, for 2 minutes, then reduce the heat to 400°F (200°C). Continue baking for another 20 to 30 minutes, or until the soufflé has risen about 2" (5 cm) above the top of the mold and the top is lightly browned. Sprinkle with confectioner's (powdered) sugar and serve at once.

Serves 4

Preparation Time: **10 minutes**
Cooking Time: **30 to 40 minutes**

CIAMBELLONE

(ITALIAN POUND CAKE)

This fine-textured cake is basic to recipes like trifle or Cassata alla Siciliana. It is also a lovely cake to serve with afternoon tea.

7 eggs

1 cup *(250 mL)* water

½ cup *(125 mL)* olive oil

1 ½ cups *(375 mL)* sugar

2 cups *(500 mL)* flour

3 tbsp. *(45 mL)* baking powder

½ cup *(125 mL)* finely chopped orange peel

*I*n a large bowl, with an electric mixer beat the eggs, water, oil and sugar on high for approximately 15 minutes.

Fold in the flour, baking powder and orange peel.

Pour into a greased 3 x 9" (8 x 23 cm) bread pan and bake for 1 hour at 350°F (180°C).

Makes: 1 cake

Preparation Time: 20 minutes
Cooking Time: 1 hour

TIRAMISÙ

As featured at Osteria de Medici, Tiramisù is a sublime creation. This luscious dessert, both rich and airy, is a fabulous flavor experience.

8 egg yolks

2 cups *(500 mL)* sugar

2 cups *(500 mL)* mascarpone cheese

4 cups *(1 L)* espresso, cold

½ cup *(125 mL)* sambuca

½ cup *(125 mL)* Marsala

½ cup *(125 mL)* amaretto

24-30 ladyfinger biscuits

*I*n a large bowl, with an electric mixer, whip the egg yolks and sugar on high speed for 30 minutes.

Add the mascarpone and 1 cup (250 mL) of cold espresso. Continue mixing for an additional 5 minutes.

Mix the remaining espresso with the liqueurs.

Dip the ladyfingers in the espresso/liqueur mixture and place 1 layer on the bottom of a 9 x 13" (23 x 33 cm) pan.

Spread half of the mascarpone mixture evenly over the ladyfingers. Add a layer of the remaining dipped ladyfingers and top with the remaining mascarpone mixture. Spread evenly. Cover and refrigerate overnight.

Before serving, garnish with grated/shaved chocolate and/or dust with cocoa powder.

Serves 6

Preparation Time: 1 hour

Pictured on page 192.

Torta Di Mele

(Apple Cake)

This very moist apple cake is fragrant and has an excellent flavor.

12 eggs

2 cups *(500 mL)* sugar

½ cup *(125 mL)* vegetable oil

3 cups *(750 mL)* all-purpose flour

2 tsp. *(10 mL)* baking powder

4 medium apples, peeled, cored, finely diced

*I*n a large bowl, with an elecrtic mixer, whip the eggs, sugar and oil on high speed until peaks form.

Slowly blend the flour and baking powder into the egg mixture.

Stir in the apples.

Pour the batter into a greased 9" (23 cm) round cake pan and bake for 45 minutes, or until cooked inside.

Let cool, then remove the cake from the pan.

Serves 12

Preparation Time: 30 minutes
Cooking Time: 1 hour

TORTA DI CITRO

(LIME CAKE)

Lively lime flavor pervades this luscious light, creamy, silky-textured dessert.

12 limes, juice of

3 limes, grated rind

24 egg yolks

6 cups (*1.5 L*) sugar

3 cups (*750 mL*) hot milk

3 tbsp. (*45 mL*) gelatin

4 cups (*1 L*) whipping cream (32% m.f.)

*I*n a double boiler, over simmering water, combine the lime juice, egg yolks and sugar and whisk steadily for 10 minutes.

Add the remaining ingredients and whisk for an additional 5 minutes.

Pour the batter into a round 9" (33 cm) cake pan and refrigerate for 4 hours.

Unmold to serve.

Serves 12

Preparation Time: 10 minutes
Cooking Time: 10 minutes

Pictured opposite.

CRÈME CARAMEL

(CARAMEL CUSTARD)

This classic dessert is a favorite in many countries. The rich caramel and creamy custard are a heavenly combination. Galliano adds a gorgeous golden color and spicy, flowery flavor.

CARAMEL

2 cups *(500 mL)* sugar

1 cup *(250 mL)* water

CUSTARD

4 eggs

¼ cup *(60 mL)* sugar

2 cups *(500 mL)* warm milk

⅓ cup *(75 mL)* Galliano liqueur

Caramel: In a saucepan combine the sugar and water. Bring to a boil, stirring constantly, until it turns a caramel color. Remove from the heat and pour the caramel evenly into 4, 1 cup (250 mL) custard cups. Refrigerate for 20 minutes, or until the caramel has hardened.

Custard: In a medium bowl, beat the eggs. Add the sugar, milk and Galliano, mixing well. Set aside.

Remove the custard cups from the refrigerator and divide the egg mixture evenly among the cups.

Set the custard cups in a baking pan with water about half the depth of the custard cups. Bake for 30 minutes at 350°F (180°C). The custard is done when it feels firm to the touch.

Remove the custard from the oven and chill in the custard cups in the refrigerator.

To serve, invert the cups onto individual plates. Serve chilled.

Serves 4

Preparation Time: 20 minutes
Cooking Time: 40 to 45 minutes

Pictured opposite.

Cassata Alla Siciliana

A traditional Easter, festival or wedding cake, this dessert has been made in Sicily for a thousand years. Candied fruit was brought to Sicily by Arab invaders and even the name has Arabic origins, quas'at, meaning in a case or mold.

1 fresh pound cake 3 x 9"
  (8 x 23 cm), see page 193

1 lb. (500 g) ricotta cheese

2 tbsp. (30 mL) heavy cream

1/4 cup (60 mL) sugar

3 tbsp. (45 mL) Strega* or an
  orange-flavored liqueur

3 tbsp. (45 mL) coarsely chopped
  mixed candied fruit

2 oz. (55 g) semisweet chocolate,
  coarsely chopped

CHOCOLATE FROSTING

12 oz. (340 g) semisweet chocolate,
  cut in small pieces

3/4 cup (175 mL) strong black coffee

1/2 lb. (250 g) unsalted butter, cut
  into 1/2" (1.5 cm) pieces,
  thoroughly chilled

With a sharp, serrated knife, slice the end crusts off the pound cake and level the top if it is rounded. Cut the cake horizontally into 1/2 to 3/4" (1.5 to 2 cm) thick slabs.

With a wooden spoon rub the ricotta through a coarse sieve into a bowl and beat it with a rotary or electric beater until it is smooth. Beating constantly, add the cream, sugar and Strega. With a rubber spatula, fold in the chopped candied fruit and chocolate.

Center the bottom slab of the cake on a flat plate and spread it generouly with the ricotta mixture. Carefully place another slab of cake on top, keeping the sides and ends even, and spread with more ricotta. Repeat until all the cake slabs are reassembled and the filling has been used up – ending with a plain slice of cake on the top. Gently press the loaf together to make it as compact as possible. Do not worry if it feels wobbly; chilling firms the loaf. Refrigerate the cassata for about 2 hours, or until the ricotta is firm.

Chocolate Frosting: Melt the chocolate with the coffee in a small heavy saucepan over low heat, stirring constantly until the chocolate has completely dissolved. Remove the pan from the heat and beat in the chilled butter, 1 piece at a time. Continue beating until smooth. Chill the frosting until it thickens to spreading consistency. With a small metal spatula, spread the frosting evenly over the top, sides and ends of the cassata, swirling it decoratively. Cover loosely with plastic wrap, waxed paper or aluminum foil and let it "ripen" in the refrigerator for at least 24 hours before serving it.

Serves 8

BABIES

Let us not forget the babies, following are a few recipes for the young ones. Each recipe calls for the freshest produce and meats. After all, babies are as important as adults.

BODINO DI MELE

(PURÉED APPLES)

1 apple, peeled, cored, chopped

3 cups *(750 mL)* water

1 tsp. *(5 mL)* sugar

Variations: Substitute pears or peaches for apples

Place all of the ingredients, including the apple peelings, into a small saucepan and simmer until the apple is very soft, about 20 minutes.

Remove the apple from the pan, discarding the peelings, and purée the apple in a food processor. Refrigerate. Serve cold.

The skins are used because they contain essential vitamins.

Yield: Approximately ¾ cup (175 mL) of sauce

Preparation Time: **5 minutes**
Cooking Time: **20 minutes**

BODINO DI POLLO

(CREAMED CHICKEN)

½ chicken breast

½ medium potato, peeled

½ celery stalk

½ carrot

¼ onion

2 cups *(500 mL)* water

1 tsp. *(5 mL)* salt

2 fresh basil leaves

In a small saucepan, combine all of the ingredients and bring to a boil. Simmer until the vegetables are soft, about an hour. Remove from the pot and purée in a food processor.

Refrigerate up to 4 days.

Yield: 4 portions

Preparation Time: **5 minutes**
Cooking Time: **1 hour**

ZUCCHINI CON RISO BODINO

(ZUCCHINI & RICE PURÉE)

2 cups *(500 mL)* water

½ cup *(125 mL)* rice

2 cups *(500 mL)* chicken broth, see page 12

½ small zucchini, chopped

¼ fresh tomato, chopped

salt to taste

*I*n a small saucepan. Bring the rice and the water to a boil. Cook until the rice is cooked and all the liquid has evaporated, about 20 to 25 minutes.

In another small saucepan, bring the broth to a boil. Add the zucchini and tomato. Cook until the vegetables are soft, about 20 minutes. Add the cooked rice and purée in a food processor.

Refrigerate up to 4 days.

Yield: 4 portions

Preparation Time: 5 minutes
Cooking Time: 35 to 40 minutes

PASTINA IN BRODO

(SMALL PASTAS IN BROTH)

1 cup *(250 mL)* pastina*

2 cups *(500 mL)* chicken broth, see page 12

salt to taste

*I*n a large pot of boiling, salted water, cook the pastina until tender, about 15 minutes. Meanwhile, bring the broth to a boil and add the salt. Drain the pastina and add it to the broth.

Refrigerate up to 3 days.

Yield: 2 portions

Preparation Time: 5 minutes
Cooking Time: 15 minutes

* Pastina is any of several very small pasta shapes, stars, alphabets, etc. They are usually used in broth or soups.

CAMOMILE HERB TEA

1 quart (*1 L*) water

1 camomile tea bag

sugar to taste

*B*ring the water to a boil and add the tea bag. Let it steep for 5 minutes and add sugar to taste.

Makes 4 cups of very mild tea

CANARINO

1 quart (*1 L*) water

3 medium lemons, peel of

sugar to taste

*I*n a small saucepan. bring the water to a boil and add the lemon peel and sugar. Boil for 20 minutes.

Served hot or cold.

Makes 4 cups

These drinks are also used by those who prefer caffeine-free drinks.

SPECIAL
OCCASIONS

Menu

La Cena Di San Valentino

(St. Valentine's Dinner)

Baked Mushrooms and Scallops page 107

Pheasant with Porcini Sauce page 139

Zucchini Al Pomodoro page 167

Risotto Zaferano page 183

Fragole Semifreddo page 198

Menu
Traditional Italian Christmas Feast

Curly Endive Soup page 48

Bocconcini Tomato Salad page 63

Roast Saddle of Veal page 147

Spinach

Asparagus

Roasted Potatoes page 178

Amaretto Pears page 202

Festa Pasquale

(Easter Feast)

This special roasted lamb dish, perfumed with rosemary and garlic, is traditionally served at Easter dinner.

16 lb. *(7.5 kg)* baby lamb

2 cups *(500 mL)* olive oil

6 garlic cloves

3 tbsp. *(45 mL)* chopped rosemary

½ cup *(125 mL)* chopped parsley

salt & pepper to taste

3 cups *(750 mL)* white wine

Cut the lamb into 4 pieces. Place it in a large baking pan with the oil and bake at 400°F (200°C) for 45 minutes.

Drain off the oil and add the garlic, rosemary, parsley, salt and pepper. Continue roasting for 10 minutes.

Add the wine and roast for 35 minutes. Baste several times with the wine.

Cut the lamb into portions and serve with roasted potatoes and peas.

Serves 10 to 12

Preparation Time: **55 minutes**
Cooking Time: **1 ½ hours**

TACCHINO RIPIENO

(THANKSGIVING DINNER)

Chicken livers, garlic and Parmesan add rich flavor and aroma to this special stuffing.

10-12 lb. *(4.5 - 5.5 kg)* turkey

CHICKEN LIVER PARMESAN STUFFING

1 lb. *(500 g)* chicken liver*, cooked, chopped

4 eggs

½ cup *(125 mL)* chopped parsley

1 medium green pepper, chopped

3 cups *(750 mL)* Parmesan cheese

3 cups *(750 mL)* bread crumbs

4 garlic cloves, chopped

2 carrots, chopped

1 onion, chopped

3 tbsp. *(45 mL)* beurre manié, see page 14

3 cups *(750 mL)* white wine

Season the turkey inside and out with salt and pepper.

Combine the stuffing ingredients in a large bowl. Stuff the turkey.

Rub the turkey with oil and place in a 350°F (180°C) oven for about 30 minutes.

Add the carrots and onion to the pan and continue roasting for another 2 hours.

Drain off the fat and remove the turkey from the pan.

Place the pan on top of the stove over high heat; add the wine, thicken with beurre manié and season to taste.

Serve with red and green peppers, green beans and potatoes.

Serves 8 to 10

Preparation Time: 30 minutes
Cooking Time: 3 hours

* To cook the chicken livers, sauté them in 2 tbsp. (30 mL) of butter for a few minutes, until they are browned and the centres are just a bit pink. Do NOT overcook.

Panettone

(Christmas Bread)

This sweet bread originated in Milan. It is served at special celebrations, weddings and christenings, as well as at Christmas time.

1 cup (*250 mL*) softened butter

1 ½ cups (*375 mL*) sugar

1 tbsp. (*15 mL*) grated lemon rind

4 eggs

1 cup (*250 mL*) milk

1 tbsp. (*15 mL*) vanilla

1 tbsp. (*15 mL*) brandy

1 tbsp. (*15 mL*) rum

4 cups (*1 L*) flour

4 tsp. (*20 mL*) baking powder

1 tsp. (*5 mL*) salt

1 cup (*250 mL*) raisins

1 cup (*250 mL*) chopped citron

1 cup (*250 mL*) chopped
   maraschino cherries

1 cup (*250 mL*) chopped walnuts

*I*n a large bowl, cream together the butter and sugar, then add the lemon rind and eggs, 1 at a time, beating well after each.

Add the milk, vanilla, brandy and rum and blend well.

Sift the flour, baking powder and salt together and gradually add to the creamed mixture.

Fold in the raisins, citron, cherries and nuts until well blended.

Pour into 9" (23 cm) angel food pan and bake at 350°F (180°C) for about 1 hour. When a toothpick is inserted and comes out clean it is done.

Serves 12

Preparation Time: 30 minutes
Cooking Time: 1 hour

WINE

REGIONAL WINES

*V*albiferno – This name is used by the ancient inhabitants of the hills where the vineyards are found which produce this particular red wine. It is a ruby red color with purple tints and a pleasant bouquet. The flavor is refined, smooth, well balanced, easy to drink. It accompanies roasts and cheeses well.

*L*iburno – This wine is from a hill named Liburno near the south boundary of the Sannto district. This white wine is made from Trebbiano grapes which give it a delicate flavor and bouquet. It should be enjoyed young, at 50 to 53°F (10 to 12°C), with hors d'oeuvres, fish and cold white meats.

WINE STORAGE

*A*ll bottles of wine should be kept lying down so that the corks remain moist. This is to keep the corks from drying out and permitting air to come into contact with the contents, air is the prime enemy of wine. Dessert wines are an exception to this rule. Deterioration is prevented due to their higher alcohol content. These wines may be stored with the necks up.

BARILE WINE

This is from my father – Nicola Barile

---

17 cases grapes (each case is 42 lbs./*19 kg*)

   4 cases moscat grapes (white)

   4 cases alleganti

   3 cases barberra

   3 cases garingani

   3 cases zinfandel

Crush 2 cases of grapes and cook the pulp and juice for 5 minutes. Mix the hot grapes into the cold crushed grapes. Press the grape mixture into a large barrel called a gallon. Let it ferment for at least 6 days in a cool, dark place, 20 to 40°F (-6 to 5°C).

Pour the wine into a fresh gallon slowly, so that the sediment from the bottom does not go into the new gallon.

Fill the new container right to the neck and then add a ½" (1.3cm) of olive oil, so that the wine does not breath.

Seal with a cork and let sit for 4 months. After 4 months, open the cork and siphon the oil off of the top carefully, so that it does not mix with the wine.

The wine is now ready to drink.

Yield: 1 barrel/48 gallons (189 L)

INDEX

Share *Italian Cooking* with a friend

Italian Cooking – Great Classic Recipes _____ x $29.95 = $ _____

Shipping and handling charge (total order) _____ = $ _____5.00_____

Subtotal _____ = $ _____

In Canada add 7% GST OR 15% HST where applicable _ = $ _____

Total enclosed_____ = $ _____

U.S. and international orders payable in U.S. funds.
Price is subject to change.

NAME: _____

STREET: _____

CITY: _____ PROV./STATE_____

COUNTRY: _____ POSTAL CODE/ZIP_____

TELEPHONE: _____ FAX: _____

Please make cheque or money order payable to:

Osteria de Medici

Phone: (403) 283-5553
Fax: (403) 283-5558
antonietta@osteria.ca
www.osteria.ca

Unit 1, 201 - 10th Street N.W.
Calgary, Alberta
Canada   T2N 1V5

For fundraising or volume purchase prices, contact Osteria de Medici.

Please allow 2-3 weeks for delivery.